ADVANCE PRAISE
for

Gay, Catholic, and American
My Legal Battle for Marriage Equality and Inclusion

"Recounting confrontations with the Catholic Church to the Boy Scouts and then fighting the state of Kentucky all the way to the Supreme Court of the United States, *Gay, Catholic, and American* is the powerful story of a man and his family fighting tirelessly for positive change rooted in their belief in the fullness of charity."
—Jim Obergefell, co-author of *Love Wins*

"Greg Bourke's story is one of perseverance and tenacity, of refusing to settle for less and daring to dream big. LGBTQ Catholics and those who desire more welcoming institutions will be encouraged and inspired by reading this book."
—Michael J. O'Loughlin, national correspondent for *America: The Jesuit Review*

"The events described in this book could be seen as ordinary and unremarkable: a man finds a partner, forms a family, gets married, forges a career, and becomes a leader in his community, all while devotedly practicing his religious faith. But it becomes an extraordinary and exceptional story when you read what it took to pursue happiness, acceptance, and equality in all those arenas of his life while still remaining steadfast in that faith. In this way, Greg Bourke's *Gay, Catholic, and American* is also both universal and personal, providing a compelling read for any audience."
—Christine Becker, author of *It's the Pictures That Got Small*

"*Gay, Catholic, and American* reads as a modern 'passion' story—it is a familial and compelling story of two faith-filled men and their two children who tasted life's bittersweet moments in their unrelenting pursuit of justice, trusting in the power of faith to guide their journey and seeking to make fullness and completion in God's charity palpable in our country. This story witnesses the triumph of love and perseverance."

—Miguel Humberto Díaz, former United States ambassador to the Holy See

"In the Beatitudes, Jesus says that those who hunger and thirst for justice will be satisfied. *Gay, Catholic and American* is the story of one family's journey in that quest. Greg Bourke weaves in the struggle, fear and hope of the journey to be recognized as a family and a full participant in our society. He engagingly recounts the struggles, fears, and hopes of that journey that results in a compassion we can all learn from."

—Simone Campbell, SSS, author of *Hunger for Hope*

"*Gay, Catholic, and American* is a richly detailed memoir of Gregory Bourke's life. Throughout, the reader is struck by Bourke's conciliatory attitude toward his opponents, his unassuming tone, and his humility—despite an impressive list of accomplishments and accolades."

—Joseph Mello, author of *The Courts, the Ballot Box, and Gay Rights*

"Greg Bourke's memoir combines his and his family's journey with the paths taken by the federal judiciary toward marriage equality, his local Catholic Church toward a warm embrace of gay and lesbian couples, and the Boy Scouts toward acceptance of openly gay scoutmasters. All heartwarming stories told with charity toward all, malice toward none."

—William N. Eskridge, Jr., author of *Equality Practice*

"*Gay, Catholic, and American* is a delightfully written journey of a fellow Notre Dame gay alum. I am proud to have played a small part in his journey calling for equal rights for the LGBTQ Catholic community."

—Jack Bergen, ND '77, past chair of the Gay and Lesbian Alumni of Notre Dame and St. Mary's College

Gay, Catholic, and American

GAY,

CATHOLIC,

AND

AMERICAN

*My Legal Battle for Marriage
Equality and Inclusion*

GREG BOURKE

University of Notre Dame Press • *Notre Dame, Indiana*

Published by the University of Notre Dame Press
Notre Dame, Indiana 46556
undpress.nd.edu

Published in the United States of America

Library of Congress Control Number: 2021940099
ISBN: 978-0-268-20123-4 (Hardback)
ISBN: 978-0-268-20124-1 (Paperback)
ISBN: 978-0-268-20122-7 (WebPDF)
ISBN: 978-0-268-20125-8 (Epub)

This book is dedicated to my husband and life partner,
Michael De Leon.

It is also dedicated, like all the rest of my life works,
to God who inspired it, and to the advancement
of the Roman Catholic Church.

CONTENTS

FOREWORD

Those of you who are to have the pleasure of advancing in these pages will see sketched out an account of nearly forty years in the life of a family. A couple who met, fell in love, realized that "here at last is bone of my bone and flesh of my flesh," welcomed children, and grew and prospered as they became stalwarts of parish life and scouting activities. They spent endless days and evenings in parenting, often helped by their siblings, taking the education and security of their children seriously, and sharing responsibility for their own parents as these grew old and dependent. Along the way they acquired a wide network of friends and colleagues as they found themselves taking part in huge social and legal changes in the life of their country. And they did all this as regular and loyal Mass-attending Catholics.

When stated like that, you might well ask why this should even be the subject matter for a book. How many thousands or hundreds of thousands of families have lived or aspired to live similar lives, and never bothered to darken a publisher's door with their anecdotes? And yet what makes this a must-tell story is that the couple involved, Greg and Michael, are of the same sex. They were one of the couples whose cases led to same-sex marriage becoming legal throughout the United States. What they live and describe as a Catholic couple is something that "ought not to be," but yet very obviously is.

The deep music of the Catholic Faith and the frightened screeching of its clerical (and clericalized lay) instrumentalists are often out of whack. Luckily, as the deep music grows and becomes more audible, it becomes possible to detect quite where the clerical notes are and are not in harmony with it. One of the areas in our time where that deep music is asserting itself, and those instrumentalists are screeching, is with relation to matters LGBTQ.

So, it is indeed one of the pleasures—and reliefs—of the Bourke De Leon story to note how often ordinary Catholics at every level have been welcoming of them and their family from the beginning, with their own parents and siblings first, and then into parish life, including various forms of public parish ministry. Next, of course, during the majority of Greg's interactions with the Boy Scouts at the local level. What is anecdotal in these pages is confirmed time and time again by researchers, such as those of the Pew Foundation: the majority of Catholics have had little to no difficulty in seeing through official disapproval of LGBTQ people and of same-sex marriage. Such disapproval makes no sense once you work out that being gay or lesbian is just what some people are. And if that is the case, and we must love our neighbor as ourselves, then we must encourage them to flourish and contribute to flourishing, starting, like everybody else, from who they are.

In fact, one of the recurring sentiments in this book are the occasions where Greg fears a negative reaction, only to find that no one minds at all. There is something tremendously solid in the ordinary Catholic groundswell that held the family together as they found themselves being prepared to step into more treacherous territory, one in which we can see a vocation being forged as they begin to be confronted by the leaven of the Pharisees and of Herod. The peculiar alchemy of political and religious self-righteousness that characterizes public life in the United States was fully on display as the issue arose of whether the Boy Scouts could continue to discriminate against gay children as members, in the first place, and then against gay adults as leaders, later on. Then again when the issue became whether it was constitutional for states to ban same-sex marriage.

And here indeed Greg and his family started to confront two of the factors that came into play. On the one hand, the cowardice of those who themselves had no objection to moving forward, but also had no spine to stand up to those vehemently opposed. On the other hand, those who were triggered, by fear of the loss of a fake goodness and the security that the status quo afforded them, into genuinely threatening and hateful reaction. Some of the most chilling lines in the book are where the Bourke De Leon kids, Bryson and Isaiah, express their fears as to whether there might be gun violence at one or another public forum on the road to the decision in *Obergefell v. Hodges*. Thank heaven those fears went unrealized.

Thank heaven also that, faithful to their calling, this family was not dispirited either by the cowardly silence or by the triggered hatred. Nor were they resentful of the many slights and setbacks encountered along the way. Indeed, one of the splendid things you will pick up is how little hatred and resentment they show to those who either did nothing to help or sought to hinder. There is a beautiful moment when their archbishop treats a married gay Eucharistic minister as simply that, a Eucharistic minister, and the temperature goes down all round. A huge tribute to graciousness under fire. Those involved refused the siren calls of mutual excommunication, and the Sacrament became the sign of the kingdom rather than a weapon in a culture war.

So where to now? This book is not only a witness to something achieved and the process of achieving it in the civil sphere. It is also an important pointer to where we Catholics might take things in the future. During the period when, unbeknownst to me, Greg and Michael were living through this journey, I was sometimes asked by Catholic audiences, "Why won't the Church bless same-sex marriage?" My answer at the time was, "Bake the cake first, and then we'll worry about the flavor of the icing." By that I meant that we had at that time no history, shared memory, or living narrative of what might be the sacramental quality of same-sex couples. It would only be as we engaged fully in the political process, ensuring step by step the legal rights of same-sex couples—from pension rights to next-of-kin visiting rights to inheritance rights to citizenship rights—that it became absolutely clear that the simplest and best one-stop shop by which those rights could be assured was marriage. In addition to those rights, there is something very simple and profound that even individual U.S. states confer upon their citizens who enter into the contract of marriage: the couple gets to honor each other and be honored. For those brought up with unremitting shame about who they are, their desire, and sexual practice, such honor is huge.

But now the cake is pretty close to baked: we are starting to have a visible narrative history, shared experiences, of what it looks like for same-sex couples to want to be, and actually to get, married—and for their lives to be publicly witnessed over time. Soon a generation will be reaching adulthood for whom there was never a time when the dream of being married to someone of the same sex was impossible. These are kids for whom courtship and adolescence will have been lived through at the same age as their straight contemporaries. Kids for whom marriage will be a normal choice they might make as part of a desire to live well. So now, of course, we can begin to ask the about the icing: What is the shape of the blessing we are celebrating at the wedding of such a couple? What is it that we are giving thanks for to God as we witness the blessing God is pouring upon us in the persons and witness of this newly committed couple? Catholicism in the United States is well behind the curve on this because of its hyperpolarized Church politics, but in many countries the deep music of God's love for us is spilling out into priests and bishops, who at last are publicly encouraging the development of appropriate liturgical forms. To take this further, we need more and more widely shared witnesses to holy flourishing of the sort that Greg's family offers us in this book. The more we learn from stories like this one, the clearer it will become to us how we are to bless God for blessing us with couples whose shared lives are a blessing. That is how we will grow in discovering and enacting Catholic same-sex marriages, where it is not only the civil law honoring us but also God transforming our former shame into our promised share in God's glory.

James Alison
Catholic priest, theologian, and author
Madrid, October 2020

AUTHOR'S NOTE

The events described in this book are real and cover an extended period of time and interactions with many people over the years. My writing reflects my recollections to the best of my ability. Absolutely no malice or misrepresentation is intended whatsoever, just an honest telling of my story as I recall it. This story is presented as my own personal truth, but I also recognize that it is told from my own perspective and may vary from the perspective of others.

INTRODUCTION

Remember, Lord, your Church, spread throughout the world, and bring her to the fullness of charity, together with Francis our pope and Joseph our bishop, and all the clergy.
—Catholic Mass Eucharistic Prayer II

Charity. Charity. From the Latin, *caritas*. It was a word I'd heard a million times at Mass, but like so many others, I'd hear it once and move on without thinking. Of course you want to help people in need. Give till it hurts if you can. Be kind to yourself. All good ideas. But was that it? Were charity and *caritas* the same, or had something been lost in translation? Was there something more mysterious, maybe even mystical, going on there? I don't think I ever thought a lot about it until that one Saturday evening at Mass in the summer of 2016.

As sometimes happened during the Eucharistic Prayer, I was zoning out when our pastor, Father Scott Wimsett, came to those four words: "The fullness of charity." I'd heard them so many times before, they'd lost all meaning, but this time was somehow different. It was like I had been falling asleep at the wheel of my car while driving, and I had that sudden jerk back to alertness. I looked up to see what was going on. There was Father Scott, and there was the congregation. Nothing was out of place, nothing was unexpected. What was that all about? But I couldn't get those words out of my head. Until then they had no meaning for me. What had just happened?

Over the last few years, every week when I hear those words at Mass, they have had a similar though not quite as dramatic effect on me. For me they're a weekly wake-up call, a call to attention, to alertness, to action. At first, I didn't understand why I was having that response to such a simple phrase. In time I began to understand it was God calling me to bring a message to anyone who might want to hear about the fullness of God's love and why we should all persist at pursuing it in God's name.

In the *Catechism of the Catholic Church*, charity/*caritas* is defined as "the theological virtue by which we love God above all things for His own sake, and our neighbor as ourselves for the love of God" (no. 1822). That's quite a lot to live up to. The part of the Eucharistic Prayer most commonly used in Mass calls for all Church members to unite in a full and complete state of charity. We pray for the entire Church to be united in love. But we're tacitly acknowledging that the Church has not yet achieved a state in which we have total love for God above all things and a love for our neighbors as ourselves. Charity is something to be pursued diligently and prayerfully even as we recognize the many obstacles and barriers to a state of fullness and completion in God's love. Full charity is a mountain top too difficult to reach. That doesn't mean we shouldn't try.

Hearing those words each week serves as a reminder of my decades living openly and authentically as a gay man and a dedicated Roman Catholic. Living my life striving for the fullness of charity has taken me places I could not have imagined when I was growing up in a working-class family in Louisville, Kentucky. I never could have seen my bitter standoff and ousting by the Boy Scouts of America or my battle for same-sex marriage at the U.S. Supreme Court. The call was always there, but, as with so many people, I ignored it at times, or it was too difficult to interpret.

After prayerful reflection, I've come to realize that the Church cannot be full of charity or anything else as long as its doctrines and teachings are designed to condemn, marginalize, and push away the LGBTQ community. Each week we collectively pray for the Church to become complete in God's love and charity. We know we're not even close, but we understand it's something to which God wants us to aspire. Failure is not an option.

Beyond my fourteen years of Catholic school and more than sixty years of actively practicing my Catholic faith from the pews, I can't cite any theological credentials to write on these things. But when one feels God's persistent call to do something, it is better to forge ahead, whether you feel qualified or not. God's call can be relentless. You know God's work is much more important than anything you wanted to do for yourself, but it's not a mountain top too far.

1

EARLY YEARS—READY FOR THE '80S

In the years before my husband, Michael, and I met at the University of Kentucky (UK), I had to face and embrace my sexual orientation while trying to reconcile it with my faith. This included maintaining membership in a Catholic Church that was generally not supportive. Before I went to UK, I attended the University of Louisville (U of L) and graduated with a bachelor's in sociology. I then went on to get a master's in sociology from the University of Notre Dame. As part of my coming-out process I scheduled a few counseling sessions with the priest who'd been the chaplain at my all-male Catholic high school, Saint Xavier in Louisville. Unsure of how he would respond, I was pleasantly relieved when he reassured me that God loved and accepted me just the way I was. For a troubled nineteen-year-old coming out in 1976 and seeking that acceptance, it was the encouragement I desperately needed. It was a pivotal point in dedicating myself to finding a way to make my sexuality work with my faith and within the Catholic Church.

Michael De Leon and I met on March 20, 1982, at The Bar in Lexington, Kentucky. At the time I was twenty-four years old and had just started an MBA program at UK. Michael was twenty-three and wrapping up his bachelor's degree in agriculture at UK.

It was still against Kentucky's sodomy law to engage in "homosexual" behavior. You could get two years in prison. You couldn't fully and safely be "out" at school, at work, or at home without fear of condemnation and even potential prosecution. In those days, Kentucky had a particularly harsh, conservative Bible Belt environment that did not tolerate any perversions that deviated from collective Christian-inspired norms.

UK and Lexington in those days were both still pretty conservative and lacking even minimal tolerance for gay people. There were no LGBTQ support groups, no campus student groups, no Pride festivals. Besides a couple of other spaces where gay and lesbian people sometimes congregated, The Bar was the only semilegitimate meeting place for LGBTQ people. It was the go-to place, the only relatively safe space in an otherwise hostile environment. Beyond its doors, if you revealed your sexual orientation to the wrong person, you might lose your job or be kicked out of your apartment. You could even face physical harm.

After Michael and I met, we discovered we lived just three doors apart on South Upper Street, a few blocks from campus. That area was not a predominantly gay neighborhood by any means, so our proximity was a remarkable coincidence. It facilitated frequent visits to one another in our first weeks and months as we started dating. It was one of those sappy love-at-first-sight experiences. We'd met on a Saturday night. The next night we were back together to attend a showing of the classic movie *Streetcar Named Desire* at the Kentucky Theatre with some of Michael's other gay friends.

Within the first couple of weeks of dating, we began attending Mass together at Saint Paul the Apostle Church in downtown Lexington. I had moved to Lexington in January 1982 and was going there myself on the weekends. Michael preferred services at the Catholic Newman Center on UK's campus. Saint Paul was convenient because it was a short six-block walk from our apartments. I have always been more of a church architecture traditionalist and preferred the grand old-style church setting surrounded by statues, stained glass, burning candles, and incense. Michael enjoyed Mass at the Newman Center because it was more contemporary and the congregation was predominantly younger college students.

In reflection, it seems rather odd we would have been going out to the local gay bar on Saturday nights drinking and dancing until the wee hours of the morning, then getting up later for Sunday Mass. But that's what we did. I suppose there might have been straight couples doing the same thing, but looking back it probably was pretty extraordinary that this young gay couple was going to Catholic Mass together on Sundays in Kentucky in the early 1980s.

Our lives have always been sort of a paradox. I suppose that was just another way we didn't conform to expectations from either gay or conventional perspectives. We were not being radical or provocative; we simply chose to practice our faith together because that's how we were raised.

During our time in Lexington, we occasionally went to the Newman Center together and a few times to the Cathedral of Christ the King. Even in those days, young people liked to church-shop for one that fit with their theological beliefs and provided the right combination of comfort and spiritual satisfaction. We settled on Saint Paul the Apostle Catholic Church and thoroughly enjoyed our time there. Of course, it's not like Saint Paul had a gay ministry in those days. Michael and I simply showed up and attended services and never spoke the g-word. Don't ask, don't tell worked well in that era as we appeared to the clergy and congregation to be just another couple of college students attending Mass together. We got what we wanted and needed, but we kept a very low profile.

Both Michael and I come from what would have been considered traditional Roman Catholic families. Our parents married in the Church and practiced their faith unwaveringly from birth throughout life. Michael's parents were married forty-four years when his father, Abel De Leon Sr., passed away in 1997. My parents were married sixty-seven years when Timothy Bourke Jr. died in 2017 at age ninety-two. In our respective families, weekly attendance at Mass was mandatory. I took the traditional Catholic educational path, attending Catholic elementary and high schools and later the University of Notre Dame for graduate school. Michael went to military and public schools.

Our parents were strong role models, fully dedicated to the Catholic Church and the institution of marriage. Michael and I continued to go to Mass every week even when we left our parents' homes. We both absorbed their values as we grew up and brought them with us into our relationship together.

In those early years together, Michael and I never had an ultraserious or contentious discussion about getting or staying together forever. There were no ultimatums or threats or pleas or proposals, or anything like that.

If we had listened to societal advice from the gay or straight world, we wouldn't have even bothered trying to stay together for decades. That was against the law. It wasn't promoted in any way in the mainstream media or even in gay culture. We didn't know of any long-term gay or lesbian couples. We had no role models to steer us into what we were embarking upon. On the other hand, there were countless role models of opposite-sex couples in our families and in our parish church who valued and respected the inherent blessings of long-term committed relationships. They ended up being our role models.

Make no mistake, Michael and I had both been involved in other relationships before we met each other. When we met, we certainly didn't expect to become life partners. In the early months, our relationship was like what we southerners call "courting." It was serious but not the complete focus of our lives. That was not the world in which we lived. We were students, we both had jobs. We were working hard to achieve our respective educational goals and finding sustainable employment that would ensure our independence in adulthood. We took our relationship and our lives one day at a time. A long-term relationship just wasn't a realistic possibility. Yet, from the outset we did seem to hang out pretty much every day. We had no idea what was coming.

Then in August 1982, I had a traumatic personal experience that managed to propel our relationship to the next level. I came home one day after a long day of classes and work to find my studio apartment ransacked and burglarized. As a poor graduate student, there weren't many valuables in my apartment, but the thief stole my used black-and-white, nine-inch television and two tickets for the upcoming UK vs. LSU football game. When I walked into my apartment and saw that carnage, every drawer open and my personal belongings strewn about the floor, I remember feeling violated and shaken to the core.

My life experience to that point was based on a very quiet and safe working-class neighborhood in Louisville. I'd never experienced any type of criminal victimization. It was paralyzing at first, but after gathering my composure a bit, I walked over a few doors to Michael's apartment and he consoled me in my time of distress. I knew I could not go back to that apartment again. After talking it over, Michael and I agreed I should move in with him and his roommate, Paul, who was also gay. They had a nice two-bedroom unit on the first floor of an old house that had been converted into apartments. Having another tenant meant the monthly rent was reduced for everyone, so Paul agreed to the move.

I always think of that August 1982 episode as the time in our relationship when we made that first real commitment to one another. There were no vows or rings exchanged, just an agreement we would try living together, sharing a bedroom in a shared apartment. We did not discuss how long the arrangement might last or even if we thought it would. We just figured out we wanted to try living together and sharing our lives more completely.

Those early months were very much the honeymoon period of a relationship that many enjoy and look fondly back upon in later years. We were happy and content, broke but satisfied in doing everything we could together. Not only would we go dancing several nights a week, but we frequently enjoyed classic movies at the Kentucky Theatre. Besides attending Mass weekly, we liked "picking" at the weekend Georgetown Flea Market and tent camping and hiking at Red River Gorge in eastern Kentucky. Perhaps most memorably of all, we attended numerous UK football and basketball games together. UK students considered attendance at those games almost mandatory.

We had a small core group of gay friends we spent time with when we weren't working or pursuing our studies, but we found that as a couple in a world without couples we sometimes didn't fit into Lexington's gay scene.

Perhaps we were simply young and stupid, but we had no idea how high the odds were stacked against us as we launched our life together at that time and place. We didn't consider the lack of same-sex couple role models, the condemnation by our Church, or the legal challenges we'd face as nonmarried cohabitating adults of the same gender. Like many young people, we just didn't care. It may have been precisely that lack of concern that allowed us just enough time to shut it all out and get our relationship well-rooted before we developed greater awareness of the challenges we'd face together. We just held on tight to each other, alone, and forged ahead.

Soon after we moved in together, our extended families began to get to know each other and become intertwined. It was pretty remarkable for those days how quickly our siblings, parents, and extended family got used to us being a couple. My father was a World War II veteran, and

Michael's father was a retired U.S. Army sergeant who served in the Korean and Vietnam Wars, so those two reveled in telling their respective war stories. That common military link was something that eventually made it easier for our families to merge and develop a shared sense of family identity. Michael's sister was also a student at UK and became a frequent visitor to our apartment. There were many times we went out to yard sales with Michael's family or out to dinner with mine. Of course, whenever we could, we'd join family to attend Mass on Sundays.

Coming out to our families in Kentucky in those days, we were prepared for the possibility of rejection. By the early 1980s, we both were already into our early twenties and essentially financially independent, so that made it a little less risky. We initially did not force the issue of our sexual orientation with our families. We simply presented ourselves as a couple, and that was exactly how we were treated, fairly and equally. My parents were initially a bit apprehensive about the situation, more out of concern for me and my well-being, but we managed to allay their fears in private. It was a great gift from God that our families were so welcoming and accepting. They were remarkably supportive. What a blessing it was not having to deal with family rejection over being gay while trying to establish our relationship at the same time.

Both Michael and I grew up in relatively progressive households loyally aligned with the Democratic Party. Louisville, then as now, is the largest city in Kentucky. As the 1980s progressed, the city saw slow but growing support for gays and lesbians. Things were starting to change for the better elsewhere in the country. There was more open discussion about "gay liberation." We'd developed national leaders such as Harvey Milk. Although the media was wasn't always flattering, at least it was covering us. Painful-to-watch perpetuations of gay stereotypes at big-city Gay Pride parades gave us some visibility. In the 1960s, the public wouldn't have even known we existed. Things were moving more quickly on the East and West Coasts of the United States, but in the heartland things were changing at a snail's pace.

2

TIME IN
NEW ENGLAND

Michael and I came from modest working-class families. We both needed to work to pay our tuition and living expenses at college. Michael worked a well-paying job at UPS in Lexington loading trucks in the evening, while I worked in marketing for the Irving B. Moore Corporation, an industrial rubber manufacturer and distributor. My part-time position was arranged as an internship through the MBA program, and I continued working there after the internship ended. The company was dominated by non-college-educated employees and management, and they thought that with my background and education I could bring some needed skills and new ideas to the industrial company.

As I wrapped up my MBA program in May 1983, I began a job search focusing on the Louisville and Lexington areas. At that point in history, the U.S. and Kentucky economies were in recession, unemployment was high, and none of my graduating classmates were getting any job offers. Things were pretty bleak both nationally and in Kentucky. But Irving B. Moore Corporation came to the rescue and asked me to move to its Hartford, Connecticut, division to assume the newly created position of marketing director.

Move to Connecticut? At this decision point, Michael and I faced the first real challenge to the future of our relationship. We talked about the situation and opportunity that presented itself. We had already been living together for more than nine months, so he didn't really hesitate when I asked him if he wanted to come along with me on this bold adventure. The hardest parts were knowing that he wouldn't have a job when he got there and would have to move far away from his family and friends in Kentucky. We either had to make the major commitment of keeping the relationship going or taking the opportunity to go our separate directions. I don't remember any fights or tears or even long conversations about that decision. There really wasn't much of a decision to make. In July 1983 we loaded up a rental Ryder truck with all our fabulous tragic college home furnishings and started that long drive up to our new apartment in Connecticut.

When we arrived, we didn't know a soul. My only contacts were with people at my place of employment. Although Connecticut was already infinitely more progressive than Kentucky back in 1983, I just wasn't ready to be fully out of the closet at work and face potential harassment and discrimination. Michael, with his freshly minted degree in agriculture from UK, swiftly found employment as a representative for *New England Country Folks*, a New York-based publication for which he worked remotely. It required him to travel all over New England to call primarily on farm equipment distributors. It wasn't a great job, but it afforded him a great deal of freedom, and he got to travel all over the beautiful New England countryside.

Our experience was much like many young couples who have graduated college and moved away to launch careers in another part of the country. We were young and free and would take off on excursions whenever we could get time away from our jobs. Without a base of friends and family locally, we spent our entire lives together, exploring our new world and making plans for the future. We could go on day or weekend trips to New York City, Boston, the Berkshires, Cape Cod, the Maine coast. There were so many wonderful and romantic possibilities.

One of the outstanding things about Connecticut was that shortly after arriving we learned that Hartford had a chapter of Dignity, a Catholic LGBTQ organization that was not officially recognized by the Church. I had read about Dignity over the years before moving to Connecticut, but I didn't know of any chapters in Kentucky or close by that I could investigate. After we settled into our apartment in New Britain, Connecticut, just outside Hartford, we made plans to attend our first Mass at a Dignity meeting.

We pulled up to the location in the dark of night and I thought, this can't be the place. It was a dismal building in an old section of Hartford. But when we entered the basement meeting space, we found a small group of people who were most welcoming. They quickly made us feel at home. The masses there were conducted by priests who had either willingly or unwillingly left their official ministries with the Catholic Church. These were our first experiences expressing our Catholic faith together with other open gay and lesbian people. In 1983, that was a new and incredibly rewarding experience for both Michael and me since such an experience was inconceivable back in Kentucky.

Over those first few months in Connecticut, we made many new gay and lesbian friends by attending regular Dignity masses. We participated in cookouts, dinner parties, and prayer services. Another remarkable development: we finally made friends with some other Catholic gay couples who like us were in exclusive and committed relationships. We became very good friends with one couple, Andrew Beck and Gary Cushing, who were just a few years older. They became couple-mentors, and we shared much food, drink, travels, and worship. We also attended one of Dignity's inspirational weekend religious retreats in the Connecticut hills. We shared faith and fellowship with the Dignity Hartford members, and this led to some incredible lifelong friendships. Our association with Dignity provided us a sense of gay community and nurtured our spiritual needs as gay Catholics.

After the one-year lease at our suburban New Britain apartment complex expired, we decided we wanted to move closer to the city, so we took a second-floor apartment in an old three-story Victorian house that had been converted into apartments. The old-Hartford neighborhood off Farmington Avenue was in the early stages of regentrification, but crime was rampant. It was not uncommon from our window to see prostitutes standing on the street corner. Our apartment and cars were burglarized, but the house and apartment were beautiful and historic. In addition, the neighborhood was full of gay people, which provided us with our first experience living in a largely gay community. Another advantage was the magnificent Cathedral of Saint Joseph in Hartford, which was about a two-block walk from our place. This became our Sunday go-to location for Mass when we didn't want to wait until Sunday night for a Dignity service. By this point, Michael was seeking a career redirection and started working on a certificate in computer programming at the Computer Processing Institute.

During this period, the AIDS epidemic started escalating. Both the media and the gay community began paying more attention to it. The media gave abundant coverage to the crisis, mostly generating fear and loathing of gay people. Worse, the realities of people we knew falling ill and dying were plentiful and heart-wrenching. It was a terrible, fearful time because everyone seemed to blame gay people for the epidemic, and no one had a clue how to stop it. Like many gay people who lived to survive that terrible era, I often have survivor guilt. I sometimes wonder why so many wonderful friends were taken but some of us were spared.

After one year of street sounds and city life in Hartford, I learned of a rental coming available through one of my co-workers. It was the first floor of a multifamily house in sleepy, suburban West Hartford. Only a couple of miles from where I was working in Newington, this place offered location, serenity, and convenience. Michael had begun working as a computer programmer at Aetna, just down the street from our new apartment. That job launched what would become his lifelong career in information technology. The apartment in West Hartford was perfect for both of us. We loved the quiet neighborhood and enjoyed long walks talking and gawking at the diverse architecture. The two years we spent in that apartment were some of our most enjoyable together.

After we moved to West Hartford, Mass at the downtown cathedral was no longer convenient. Through our ongoing affiliation with some of the folks at Dignity we began to learn of the many closeted Catholic priests in the Hartford area. After learning one of them, Father Caesar Perotti, was co-pastor at St. Mark the Evangelist Catholic Church close to our residence, we attended Mass there and eventually joined the parish. We became friends with Father Perotti and enjoyed attending his dinner parties and cookouts at the parish rectory, often with other gay men and a few other closeted gay priests. That friendship developed into holiday trips out to Cape Cod that included Father Perotti and some of our other gay friends. Going to Mass at St. Mark's was convenient for us, and we also felt very comfortable attending services led by a priest who we knew was gay and who was comfortable with both his sexual orientation and his call to ministry.

3

MY OLD KENTUCKY HOME AGAIN

After about four years in Connecticut, traveling home to Kentucky for holidays, weddings, funerals, and vacations, we began to think more and more about moving back home to be closer to our families. Actually, after about five years of renting together we began to consider the financial benefits of buying a house. As a young couple in the pricey Connecticut market we would have found that to be a huge stretch in 1987. We knew that back in Kentucky the average cost of a house was about a third of that in Connecticut. Deciding the time was good for both of us to make a move, we initiated long-distance job searches. Thankfully, by 1987 the recession had eased a bit. Given my experience in industrial marketing, I was offered a job at Brandeis Machinery in Louisville, and Michael landed a job in computer programming with Humana. We reluctantly said goodbye to our jobs and friends in Connecticut and loaded up another rental truck to move back to Kentucky.

Briefly in that late summer of 1987, Michael and I moved in with my parents, who had an empty nest at that point. My father had retired and was pretty laid back about it all, and my mother seemed thrilled to have people in the house for which she could cook big meals once again. It was a little strange for Michael and me to move into my old room and sleep together in my childhood bed, but we knew it was only a temporary stay.

My aunt, Gaye Bourke, was a local realtor, and everyone in my big Catholic extended family used her for real estate transactions. So we contacted her to launch a house search. We looked at a couple of properties in south Louisville close to my parents, but they weren't close to where I was working at the industrial park in suburban Jeffersontown, and Michael was working downtown.

Aunt Gaye finally pitched us a house in the near-suburban area of Saint Matthews. It was close to an interstate and about halfway between our places of employment. Built in 1939, it was vacant and on the market to settle the estate of the original owner, a widow who'd been living alone for twenty years before passing. She was its first and only owner. Needless to say, the place needed extensive renovation and updating. Luckily, my retired father, the ultimate handyman (his nickname was "Pliers") was more than willing to come help us do much of the work. We gave him his own key. He spent countless hours painting and doing electrical and plumbing work. Often we would come home from our jobs and find him at work, sometimes with both my mother and food waiting for us.

As we were settling back into Kentucky life with our new jobs and new old house, the next step was for us to find a church and parish that suited our needs. If you couldn't tell from some of my previous comments, convenience was often an important factor in our decisions. We investigated the closest Catholic church, Our Lady of Lourdes, which was less than two blocks away. When we first attended Mass there, it was pretty much what we expected and what anyone would expect from a Catholic parish in Kentucky in 1987: conservative and very traditional. Michael and I started to attend Mass together there, but we stayed under the radar and mostly invisible.

After a few services at Lourdes, we decided to register with the parish, so we called the parish center and set up an appointment. We presented ourselves together at the rectory to register with a young, new associate priest, Father Wayne Crabtree. The encounter was mostly a simple paper-processing transaction with no mention of us being gay or a couple, just a shake of hands and pass the paperwork. We also had a brief discussion about our respective experiences as Catholics, verifying that we had all of our sacraments, which would have been expected if we wanted to qualify for membership. (Father Wayne left the parish in 1990 and shortly thereafter also left the priesthood. In 2020, he is openly gay and living in Louisville.)

After Michael and I registered in the parish in 1987, we became regulars there. Because of the cultural climate, we felt it was best to keep a low profile, which we did for many years. We had a taste of being openly gay and Catholic at St. Mark's in West Hartford and with Dignity in Connecticut, so it was a little stifling to be back in a traditional Catholic Church environment where we could not bring our whole selves to church. At this point in my life I had been out of the closet for more than ten years and was finding it increasingly difficult to justify not being open and honest about who I was all the time with everyone I encountered.

Acting out of frustration, I decided it was necessary for me to have a sit-down talk with our pastor at that time, Father Robert Osborne. I scheduled a meeting with him at the parish center and went in to have an official coming-out meeting.

When I entered his office, Father Oz, as he was affectionately known by his parishioners, totally soothed my fears and concerns with his gentle smile and welcoming demeanor. He had no idea what I wanted to talk about. I suppose that is often the case when a priest makes an appointment with a parishioner. Father Oz could have thought I needed counseling or was dealing with a truly dreadful situation or a crisis of spirituality. Instead I explained to him that Michael and I were a gay couple and had been for more than five years at that point, and we simply wanted to know if we would continue to be welcome in his parish.

There was no hesitation whatsoever. Father Oz reassured me we would most certainly be welcome. He did not present any stipulations or special conditions. He just told me that of course we would be welcome. I'm not sure what I expected, but that was the most compassionate response I could have received at that time. In reflection now, I have to be thankful once again for God's blessings that under those circumstances he provided me a messenger that told me exactly what I needed to hear.

For many years thereafter, with our busy work and family life, we remained relatively invisible at church, occasionally signing up to volunteer for parish-sponsored events. Each summer for many years we volunteered at the bratwurst booth sponsored by Lourdes at the big granddaddy of summer church picnics in Louisville, the Saint Joseph

Orphan's Picnic. This provided some of our closest nonchurch interaction with some of our fellow parishioners. Frequently we took advantage of the opportunity to out ourselves. Going to Mass each week and rushing home right after did not provide us with an opportunity to become widely known in the parish as a gay couple. Of course, over time the word started to spread, but it honestly did not appear to make a bit of difference to anyone.

It is fair for readers to ask, Why did it work for us at Lourdes at first and for all these years? That is a difficult question that's open to speculation. We never publicly forced our sexual orientation or relationship on our fellow parishioners. Southern folk do like to gossip and talk, and certainly there was some of that, but they are also often reluctant to confront others. Michael and I didn't ask for favors or special recognition. We just showed up for Mass and delivered our check weekly in the collection basket, as was expected of all parish members. People got to see us and know us. We were so engrained in the community before we ever developed a public identity as activists. We were simply another couple in the pews, showing up and doing the work. For many Catholics that is what makes up the Church.

The world was so different in those days in many respects. Volunteerism and church ministry engagement were not as prominent as they have become in the twenty-first century. My father used to always pass along to me advice that he had gained while serving in World War II: never volunteer for anything! With our corporate jobs, keeping up with our parents and extended families, and updating and maintaining our needy old 1930s home, we really didn't have time to do much more at the parish other than attend services each weekend. That was enough for us during the late 1980s and through most of the 1990s.

That changed in late 1996 when I received a calling to sign up for a volunteer ministry. Lourdes practices stewardship and does not charge tuition in its parish elementary school, but it does expect all parishioners to contribute as much time, talent, and treasure as they can to support its stewardship model. Michael and I were already donating generously financially, but after countless appeals by parish staff to all parishioners to get involved in other ministries, I relented and signed up for training to become a Communion minister. I was a little concerned at first. Although I felt accepted by my fellow parishioners while sitting anonymously in the pews, I wasn't sure how they'd react to having me standing in front of the Communion line distributing the precious body and blood of Christ. My fears ran away with me. Would people snub me, make some kind of gesture of indignation, or complain to the staff about my new role? When I first started serving, and for the first couple of years, I had constant anxiety that someone would cause a scene, or I'd be called to the pastor's office to be relieved from duty. Now, more than twenty years later, I can tell you I've continued in this ministry and have never had a problem.

4

FAMILY MATTERS

Several very important events occurred in the mid- to late 1990s that dramatically changed our outlook toward work and life. First, Michael and I made an early lump-sum payment in March 1998 to pay off the outstanding mortgage on our house. We had taken a fifteen-year mortgage when we purchased the house in 1987, hoping to retire that debt as soon as possible, and we worked toward that goal diligently. Knowing that we still had that debt (and only that debt) hanging over us, it was tremendously liberating to be able to pay it off. Although we were selectively out and open with co-workers, Michael at General Electric and I at Humana, about our relationship and sexual orientation, there were no LGBTQ protections yet against workplace discrimination. At work we had revealed our relationship only on a need-to-know basis. Paying off the mortgage early gave us tremendous relief and freedom in our personal lives and left us more willing to test the boundaries at work.

Around this same time, in January 1999, the city of Louisville passed its Fairness Ordinance, which secured legal protection from LGBTQ employment discrimination. It was the very first piece of pro-LGBTQ legislation ever passed in Kentucky. That hard-fought win took many years of strategizing and challenging work, but it validated the changing opinions of Louisville residents, who began to acknowledge LGBTQ protections were needed to prevent future discrimination. The debate that swept through the city was lively and progressive by Kentucky standards and for that period. Michael and I were comforted and emboldened after the law passed, which meant that after many years with our respective corporate employers we finally had protection from discrimination against us in the workplace based on our sexual orientation.

During this same period, Michael's father, Abel De Leon Sr., was suddenly and unexpectedly diagnosed with colon cancer at age sixty-three. Abel had long since retired from the U.S. Army and had been working as a social worker at Fort Knox, Kentucky, in a civil servant job. He and Michael's mother were both civil servants and were preparing for retirement when fate dealt them and us a great blow. Abel stopped working and went on medical leave after receiving the diagnosis while he began chemotherapy. Michael spent every spare minute he could away from work to make the one-hour drive down to the family farm in Rineyville to help with whatever needed to be done. His father fought the brave fight, and during that time Michael and his parents drew even closer. When Abel finally passed in 1997, it was a devastating blow to the whole family, one that set a lot of other wheels in motion.

After Abel's passing, Michael's mother, Barbara, realized immediately that she could not and would not continue on at the family farm by herself. Barbara decided it would be best to sell the farm and move to Louisville so she could at least be close to us. Her other two children, Debra and Abel Jr., lived much farther away. She did not want to leave the central Kentucky area where she'd spent so much of her adult life. Barbara ended up selling the farm at auction and moving into an apartment just a few blocks away from our home. We spent an incredible amount of time together while we helped her prepare the farm for sale and move her into an apartment. Later we helped her select and move to a home she purchased just a few blocks away. Our lives became intertwined for quite some time after that. During this medical and personal period of crisis and transition, Michael and I both developed an even greater appreciation for our families, and we began to spend increasing amounts of time with them.

There was one other thing to deal with in 1997 besides the passing of Michael's father. I was facing my fortieth birthday. Michael would be right behind me the following April. His father's death had turned our attention to our own mortality, but we also came to another realization: our biological clocks were ticking. If we were ever going to have a family, the time was probably approaching.

I don't ever remember talking about kids before then, and honestly a family really wasn't an option in those days. We hadn't considered or researched surrogacy. Being gay with little nondiscrimination protection, we figured adoption would be out of the question. But we had become aware of two local same-sex couples who'd successfully adopted children, so we began to think. With us, that's always a dangerous thing.

This was a period before social media, and the Internet was in its infancy, so word traveled slowly. Gay families with children were not something heavily promoted in the LGBTQ community. Then we found out that one of the gay dads we learned about worked with Michael at GE. He provided Michael with important and confidential information about how to approach the adoption process. We learned that Kentucky law prohibited nonmarried couples from jointly adopting children; only married couples or single adults were allowed to legally adopt. If a same-sex couple wanted to adopt, only one of the partners could be the legal parent.

Michael's co-worker told us that only one private adoption agency in Kentucky, Adoptions of Kentucky, was willing to work with gay and lesbian couples to help them adopt. Early during 1998, Michael contacted the agency to set up an initial appointment. Michael and I both attended the first meeting as a couple, but we had been coached beforehand not to discuss our being a gay couple. This was assumed by the attorney, but we should not speak of it. That way the attorney handling our adoption and the agency's owner, Carolyn Arnett, would be able to claim ignorance about our being a gay couple if that issue ever arose during the legal process. How quaint that sounds today.

That initial meeting was way beyond awkward. We went into it afraid to open our mouths or reveal much at all. Although Carolyn had counseled gay clients before, it almost seemed as if this was her first time at this kind of rodeo. We were given loads of paperwork, wrote a big check to the agency, and started the whole process.

Since this was a private agency, birth mothers facing unwanted pregnancies frequently sought to have some say over the new parents. We were instructed, not by the attorney but by an office assistant, to prepare a profile of our family so we could build a case for why a prospective birth mother would want to place her child in our care. In other words, they wanted us to prepare a marketing brochure of sorts to convince a birth mother to let us adopt her child.

After we developed our portfolio, we sat back to wait for our profile to be selected. Unlike many seeking adoptions, we did not place restrictions on the race, gender, or medical condition of the child we were willing adopt. This greatly expedited the selection process. The next phase required multiple home visits and interviews by a licensed social worker to prepare a Home Study to evaluate the safety and security of our home. Michael and I openly presented ourselves to the social worker as a gay couple. Our sexual orientation was in no way a factor in the assessment for appropriateness of our home.

After we were selected by a birth mother, a meeting was arranged between the three of us in the Adoptions of Kentucky office. Despite the unusual circumstances, we all got along remarkably well. After delivery, the birth mother wanted to continue to receive regular written updates on the progress of her child and also to have occasional personal contact. As the birth mother progressed through her pregnancy, we became a bit of a social support system for her. We even transported her to the public health clinic for pregnancy checks and an ultrasound. When it came time for her to give birth, she called us to take her to the hospital. She even trusted us to watch her three-year-old son while she was in labor and in the hospital after giving birth. Over the years, we have maintained a friendly relationship with her. Our child has grown up knowing, loving, and respecting his birth mother.

There are many stories out there about birth mothers changing their minds about adoption after the baby is born, so we were anxious about this possibility. When we brought our baby, Bryson, home from the hospital, we also brought his birth mother along with us to our home to visit for a while and say goodbye before taking her back to her apartment. It was an awkward but necessary step. After we cleared that hurdle, we faced the inevitable wave of visiting family and friends who wanted to meet the new addition. They showered us with baby gifts, well-wishes, and, of course, needed parenting advice.

5

INTRODUCING THE INFANT TO OUR CHURCH

A couple of weeks after bringing our baby home, we decided it was time to take him to Sunday Mass with us.

We'd done a pretty good job of keeping a low profile in our parish up until then, but that was about to change. As is typical with us, we didn't think there'd be a problem or controversy. By mid-1999, Michael and I had already been active members of the parish for twelve years, so we felt pretty confident we were going to be safe from any type of harassment or rejection. We just assumed everything would go well. It did. When we walked in for the first time carrying our baby, suddenly everyone's radar screen lit up, but in a good way. People took notice of us. Many of them cooed over the infant and asked questions. Since then, we've had numerous people tell us they will never forget that first day we walked into church with our baby and how surprising and remarkable it was to witness.

Within a couple months we knew it was time to start the process of having the baby baptized in our church. After we saw an announcement in the weekly bulletin about a cohort scheduled for parents who needed children baptized, we contacted the parish center at Our Lady of Lourdes and registered for the training. Although we always hope for the best, by this point I was starting to wonder if the parish was going to allow us to have the baby baptized. If so, would we be permitted to present ourselves to the congregation as a couple during the service?

During the pre-baptism training and the baptism itself, nobody said a word about us. "Oh, my, Mildred, there's a gay couple having their baby baptized!" The baptism actually occurred during a regular Sunday Mass, and there were several other babies being baptized at the same service. Our extended families were there for the baptism, and we had the obligatory big family baptism party at our house after the Mass. It was a very good day.

In those early days of parenting, we arranged to take time off from our jobs for the transition. Shortly thereafter we started Bryson in day care at Saint Joseph Child Development Center (CDC), a nearby Catholic-sponsored day care that was well regarded. Again, we braced ourselves for potential rejection, not knowing if the Catholic organization would allow a gay couple to have a child enrolled. After meeting with the director of the CDC and discussing our unique situation, we all agreed that our child and our family would be welcome and well cared for at the center.

Michael and I returned to work, and we adjusted to having a baby in the house and in our constant care. It was not easy, but we received extensive advice and assistance from our families. They spent a lot of time at our house now that we had the attraction of a baby. We also took him to Mass each Sunday and never experienced a hint of controversy or criticism from our fellow parishioners or the clergy or staff at Lourdes.

Before Bryson reached the age of one, Michael and I escalated talks about adding another child to the family, and so we contacted Adoptions of Kentucky to initiate the process again. As was the case with our first child, we expressed a preference for an infant and expected it to take up to a year before a suitable match might take place. To our surprise, within a few weeks after completing the preliminary paperwork, we got a call from the agency. We were told that although we had expressed an interest in another newborn, the agency had just received contact from a birth mother wanting to place her nearly three-year-old son.

Initially Michael and I were noncommittal. Michael's sister was a social worker who had worked on adoptions. She cautioned us about taking on an older child because they often have experienced trauma and abuse that can result in very challenging complications. At the time the agency contacted us, the child was placed in a foster home in Lexington, more than an hour away. Michael and I agreed to meet the child and evaluate whether or not to pursue adoption. We drove to Lexington with great trepidation. We feared that taking on an older child was going to be too much. But when we arrived, we met a charming little bundle of energy that won our hearts and ultimately became our second adopted child, Isaiah.

Isaiah did come with some developmental issues that required occupational therapy and other therapy, but what the heck? Just a few days after Isaiah's third birthday, he joined our family and we started the adjustment process. It was difficult. Bryson was only about eighteen months old, so our lives grew hectic. Our parenting duties expanded exponentially. Fortunately, Isaiah was able to obtain therapy through the Saint Joseph CDC where we were able to also enroll him for day care.

Within a few months, it was time for another baptism at church, so we contacted the parish. We were concerned that Isaiah's volatile behavior would create issues if we had him baptized during a regular Sunday Mass, so our pastor proposed to have a private baptism just for friends and family.

From that point on for many years we were just like any other family at church each week with our kids. We had the occasional exit from Mass to the cry room and for time-outs with antsy toddlers, but for the most part we were church regulars. Everyone at Lourdes gradually got used to seeing our alternative family there together. How amazing is that?

6

THE FREEDOM
TO MARRY

After a couple of years passed, it was time to move the kids from day care to preschool. Lourdes not only sponsored a splendid parish elementary school, but it also offered a preschool program. We moved both our kids from Saint Joseph CDC to the Lourdes preschool in August 2003. In doing so, we had to face concerns again about how they would be treated as the children of a gay couple attending a Catholic-sponsored school. Thankfully, for the next eleven years our kids attended the Lourdes parish school without significant controversy or complaint.

One of the concessions we did have to make as we built our family was that because Kentucky did not allow unmarried couples to co-adopt, we could only have one person identified as the legal parent on our children's birth certificates. Since Michael was working for an employer with more generous adoption benefits, we decided he would be the adoptive parent for both of our children. This was a source of concern to me in those early days of parenting because I knew that if something were to happen to Michael and he experienced an untimely passing, I'd be left in legal limbo. As far as Kentucky law was concerned, I had no relationship with them. We were legal strangers.

In our early days of parenting we met with our attorney and drew up a range of documents that established me as a legal guardian and healthcare surrogate to our kids. Michael's last will and testament was also amended to include language that expressed his wishes that if something happened to him, the kids should be placed in my care. Of course, there were no guarantees that would be honored in court, especially if anyone chose to contest it, but it was about the best we could do in Kentucky in those days.

The state of Kentucky saw Michael and me as legal strangers, so we had our attorney arrange other legal protections, such as durable powers of attorney and healthcare powers of attorney, so we could have some virtual privileges of marriage. Our attorney was an out lesbian in a same-sex relationship, so she helped guide us to the highest legal protection available absent the option of legal marriage. Over our thirty-three years together before our marriage was finally legally recognized in our home state, Michael and I spent many thousands of dollars on legal fees just hedging our bets and having legal documents prepared, notarized, filed, and frequently revised just so that, if necessary, we would have some of the basic rights that legally married couples take for granted.

By the start of the twenty-first century, the issue of same-sex partner health benefits had come to the fore on the national scene. Several states started offering "civil unions," which gave same-sex partners limited expansion of marriage-like recognition and privileges. Court cases and legislatures in more progressive states were moving toward legal recognition of same-sex marriage. There was of course great opposition both within those states and in more conservative states in the Midwest and the South. During the election season of 2004, eleven states voted for laws or constitutional amendments banning same-sex marriage: Arkansas, Georgia, Kentucky, Michigan, Mississippi, Montana, North Dakota, Ohio, Oklahoma, Oregon, and Utah. In Kentucky, 75 percent of voters cast their ballots for Kentucky's constitutional amendment defining marriage as between one man and one woman.

For about a year before that vote, there was a very nasty debate in Kentucky over why this constitutional amendment was necessary to ban forever same-sex marriage. In my opinion, this was perhaps the darkest period in Kentucky's long LGBTQ history. It was open season on gay people. Homophobia and discrimination were on full display. Most people in the commonwealth didn't see a problem.

There were some progressive Kentuckians who fought fiercely against the amendment, particularly our local LGBTQ rights organization, the Fairness Campaign. Michael and I proudly and defiantly displayed a Fairness Campaign yard sign that urged people to "Vote No to the Amendment," but that sign was stolen from our front yard. Twice. We feared a bit for our safety, but knew how important it was to stand up and resist the wave that was coming to beat down the LGBTQ population just as we were starting to see progress for marriage equality and other protections throughout the country.

Late 2003 and early 2004 was simply a dreadful period to be an openly LGBTQ person in Kentucky. Michael and I felt vulnerable, frightened, and dismayed. That was one of a few times in our lives we talked about moving to another part of the country where we could live our lives safely and openly, where we'd be tolerated. Feeling like our backs were against the wall, we found the resolve to double down and recommit to the fight. This was our state too, and we deserved to be here as much as any other Kentuckian. We concluded we had an obligation to stay and fight for our freedom and protection and for future generations against hateful people who would target us for exclusion from marriage equality.

After twenty-two years of "cohabitating," we thought it was important to confront the anti–gay marriage sentiment at home and throughout most of the country by taking a leap of faith that someday our marriage would actually be recognized in our home state. Around Christmas 2003, we decided the best way to counter the hateful climate in Kentucky was to do something dramatic. So we prepared to travel to the only place in North America at that time where we could get legally married: Ontario, Canada. We'd already been living together for twenty-two years and had two adopted children. We needed to make it all legal.

We started researching and planning how to get married in Canada. We figured out what to do in advance of the trip and what to do upon our arrival. The legal registration process had to be complete before the ceremony. Since we both worked, and with one kid in kindergarten and another in preschool, the calendar seemed to point us to a spring break trip.

We researched marriage venues that were same-sex friendly and settled on a lovely elevated tower that hovered over—you guessed it— Niagara Falls. Our desire was to have a marriage ceremony as traditional in vows as they could possibly be, so we used the kind of standard wedding vows you hear in the movies all the time. If we could have had a Catholic priest conduct the service, we would have done that, but it was

2004. There were very few "religious" folks who wanted to be associated with that kind of thing. Luckily, we found a wonderful Unitarian minister in Ontario, Doreen Peever, who agreed to be the celebrant.

Because it was a destination wedding, and we were planning on spending our family spring break sightseeing in Niagara Falls the rest of the week, we didn't invite many friends or family to join us. My parents were already advanced in age (seventy-eight and eighty) and making that nine-hour car trip did not appeal to or make sense for them. Michael's mother was a little younger and healthier and lived just a few blocks away, so she was all-in for the event and trip to Canada. Michael's sister was living in Georgia and had school-age children, but she decided she couldn't miss it and flew into Ontario for a few days to join us.

Our kids attended the wedding and participated in the ceremony. Their attendance was very important to us. Even at ages five and six they were aware that their parents were getting married. We hired a wedding photographer to take pictures to record the day for posterity. As we gathered at the top of that platform high over Niagara Falls on a clear sunny day, we were struck by the serendipity of the beautiful rainbow looming over the falls. They probably have rainbows every day because of those massive falls and the spraying water, but for that one day that rainbow was ours and no one else's.

Marriage means different things to different people. There are legal aspects, social aspects, financial aspects, personal rewards and benefits. In going to Canada to get legally married, we were making a statement that legal recognition of marriage is important in our culture. As forces in our state mounted efforts to make sure we could never get married legally there, we knew that legal recognition was extremely important for the benefits and privileges that come with that social and legal status.

But marriage to us was more than just a legal status. It was the best way we could formally express our love for each other and make a statement about our lasting commitment. It was also about family and the security it could afford our children by having legally married parents. Finally, marriage is, after all, a sacrament, performed in the presence of God with his blessing upon the union. Michael and I have no doubt that God was present at our wedding and fully acknowledged our marriage as sacramental and not just ceremonial. On that day, I know we enjoyed the full blessing of God upon our marriage.

7

MARRIED WITH CHILDREN

After getting married in Canada, we returned home to Kentucky, where little changed in our day-to-day lives. When the kids reached preschool age, they started participating in athletic programs with the Louisville YMCA, and we took on the role of soccer dads. They started with soccer and played that sport through the Y for a couple of years until they became eligible to play soccer in first grade at Our Lady of Lourdes. They also played volleyball, basketball, and flag football at Lourdes in their early years of elementary school. For a couple of those soccer seasons, Michael served as team coach. Again, we thought we might get some kind of protest by a parent objecting to an openly gay person as soccer coach at a Catholic school team. Those fears proved unwarranted. Both parents and soccer players accepted Michael and appreciated his efforts.

Meanwhile, as my service as a Communion minister continued, I'd developed a reputation for being quite dependable in a ministry where participants sometimes aren't. Mary Ann Holl, chair of the Lourdes Worship Committee, asked me to take over as coordinator of the Communion Ministry. Mary Ann was unmarried and retired from her corporate job as a career computer programmer at GE. I always suspected she might be a closeted lesbian, but she never came out to me. She was well aware of my status as openly gay; it was never an issue with her. In fact, that might have been her motivation in asking me to heighten my visibility with this leadership opportunity. When she asked me to take over the ministry, I wondered if she really wanted to take a chance like that. More importantly, I worried about how other parishioners might react to this further validation of my liturgical role.

After praying on it for the next few days, I gradually decided that if the Worship Committee thought I was the best person for the job, there was no choice but to take it on. That turned into a four-year run, during which I scheduled every Communion minister and trained an army of new ones.

At our monthly meetings, we planned all aspects of our worship services, from art and environment to music selections. Additional volunteer service was expected to support other parish ministries. That could mean everything from serving donuts some Sundays after Mass, helping decorate the church for Christmas, serving at parish-hosted events, organizing parish mission support, and a range of other activities. It turned out to be a productive way to enhance my image in the parish and provided me much more exposure to new and different groups of parishioners.

During this same period, Michael decided he'd volunteer to serve on the Parish Council. He held that position for several years, eventually rising to vice chair. With the advent of our becoming a "school family," we seemed to just get pulled deeper and deeper into parish ministries through the years. As we did, our concerns about being openly gay gradually faded away.

8

SCOUTING

During the start of Isaiah's first-grade year at Lourdes in 2003, he came home with a flyer from the Cub Scout pack indicating they were going to have an informational and membership recruitment meeting. Isaiah said several of his friends from school were going to join. But Michael and I were aware of the Boy Scouts of America policy prohibiting gay youth and gay adult members. We discouraged Isaiah from joining, and he was disappointed, but he didn't press the issue because he was already plenty engaged in athletic programs at the school.

But then the following year when Isaiah started second grade, he came home again with another flyer about joining Cub Scouts and really pressured us about joining. Isaiah spoke of the exciting activities his friends had experienced in scouting, such as camping, archery, and various outdoors programs. We were still reluctant to let him join but decided that since he wanted to so badly, it was probably harmless to let him join. Whatever potential inappropriate messaging he might be exposed to in Cub Scouts, we'd be able to counter and correct at home.

What we did not comprehend was that in those very early levels of Cub scouting, parents were required to be there and participate with their sons for all activities. Very soon there were monthly pack meetings, monthly den meetings, and other frequent outings and events that had us tagging along. Michael took the lead initially as the accompanying parent with Isaiah, but I also filled in whenever necessary.

At the start of Isaiah's third year of elementary school in 2005, the adult Cub Scout leader who'd been leading his den decided he could no longer carry on. As is often the case in scouting, new leaders are born out of these times of crisis when an existing leader backs away. In response to this particular challenge, several of the Cub Scout parents decided they would split up the scouting events for the coming year and have broad and shared parental leadership. That model worked relatively well for most of the school year, but later in the year it was pretty clear that the den needed a dedicated and trained leader to take over. Guess what? Andy Lyons, Troop 325's Cubmaster, approached me about it. Andy had known our family from Lourdes for many years. He knew I was a former Scout and had a passion for scouting, but more importantly he knew that if the den didn't get a new leader, it would probably be dissolved completely at the end of the school year. He'd asked me on a few occasions before to take over as leader, but I quickly brushed the idea to the side. But Andy wasn't anything if not persistent.

9

BACK IN THE CLOSET

After several more entreaties, I finally I agreed. It was one of the boldest decisions of my life. I decided to register as an adult leader with the Boy Scouts of America (BSA).

The move required that I start the BSA leader training process with its many phases of applications. Becoming a fully trained leader requires background checks, character recommendations, extensive outdoor program training, youth protection training, and on and on. But in order to serve, I had to make another decision. Even though I'd been for the most part openly gay since I was nineteen, at age forty-eight I was going to have to go back into the closet. This required a dramatic psychological shift on my part.

Before training started, the other Cub Scout parents were all aware that Michael and I were a gay couple. They'd grown comfortable with the idea of trusting me as a leader for their sons. The other parents knew I'd been a Boy Scout myself and had foundational scouting knowledge that many of them lacked. There was also safety and comfort in knowing that parents would be required to attend and participate in our den activities with the young Cub Scouts.

When I submitted my standard adult BSA application form, it required a couple of signatures. I completed my portion of the form with my signature and then submitted it to an official from our BSA unit who was qualified to sign my application. I studied that BSA form carefully. At no place was there a question about sexual orientation. There was no place provided to self-identify as gay even if I wanted to. So I signed my form and sent it to the Cubmaster, Andy Lyons, who signed it and presented it to our sponsoring organization, Our Lady of Lourdes Church, for a signature.

The parish office has a representative who's authorized to sign off on these forms. I have been told that sometimes the pastor of our church provides the signature from the sponsoring organization. I'm not sure who signed my form, but whoever it was knew I was openly gay yet didn't consider it a barrier. After that, my application form went to the district office at the Lincoln Heritage Council for final processing. The Lincoln Heritage Council (LHC) is one of nearly 300 local Scout councils nationwide that administer Boy Scouts of America programs. The LHC provided the final membership approval for all applicants in its sixty-four-county service area, and that was essentially a rubber stamp signature. If and when the background check comes through to clear the applicant, one can start the process of becoming a trained and registered adult leader.

After submitting the application form, I kept waiting and wondering if anyone would raise the issue of my sexual orientation. Would they ask if I was aware of their policies on gays in leadership positions? But they never asked.

Having completed initial online research on the required training, I signed up for an Introduction to Scout Leadership Training class at the Westport Road Church of Christ. When I walked in, I noticed it was an all-male class of about ten people. The training would last half a day. It was pretty basic, just going over the structure of the BSA and explaining its sponsoring organization structure and standards.

There was also an abbreviated Youth Protection Training session that day. We viewed a video that the trainer frequently stopped for discussion, questions, and clarifications. It contained several theatrical episodes of young Scouts being misled and exploited physically by lecherous male predators. I was crawling in my skin as I watched these videos. I felt so uncomfortable, as if everyone was looking at me and accusing me of being one of these predators. Under the circumstances I just kept my eyes forward and my mouth shut until the training was over.

The Catholic Church had been rocked by many horrific cases of clergy abuse of youth. It had reached a particularly fevered state in Louisville after the $25 million settlement in 2003 made by the Archdiocese of Louisville to resolve clergy abuse cases. The BSA also had a history of covering up sex abuse of youth by adult leaders. As a result, the BSA was growing increasingly worried about its legal liability in settling pending and future cases and containing the growing negative press coverage.

The BSA, then and still now, requires adult leaders to complete annual Youth Protection Training. This was something I always complied with in my many years as an adult Scout leader. In addition to regular training, the BSA protects youth by requiring that adult leaders follow two guiding policies: (1) "two-deep leadership," and (2) "no one-on-one contact."

The first mandates that for every Scout activity or outing, at least two adult leaders must be present. Activities cannot occur if at least two adults are not secured in advance for the protection of the youth and the adult leaders. The second policy prohibits instances where just one youth is in the company of just one adult. Again, if this situation occurs, it puts both the youth and adult leader at risk. These two policies protect youth from abuse and adults from potentially false accusations. In my many years as a Scout leader, I completed this training as required every year and vigilantly enforced these rules, not just to protect the Scouts but, more so, myself.

My greatest fear was that one of the boys at some point might raise a false allegation of improper behavior against me. If you know preteen or teenage boys, you know they can do some pretty mischievous things, sometimes intentionally and other times unintentionally. What if one of these boys who knew I was gay decided to have some "fun," or be downright malicious, and accuse me of behaving inappropriately or even illegally? I often feared such a thing might happen.

Sometimes during those long nights camping with the troop, I lay in my sleeping bag staring at the top of my tent and worrying about it as I tried to get some sleep. Although this never happened, that heightened concern kept me extravigilant about enforcing the Scout policies of two-deep leadership and no one-on-one contact. I needed to protect myself from even the slightest suggestion of improper behavior. It was a heavy burden and a worry for me, one that I don't think other Scout leaders had to bear quite so heavily.

The full BSA adult leader training also required several other classes, including one called Outdoor Leader Essentials. I had to spend a weekend at a regional BSA property, Camp Crooked Creek, to get schooled with other wannabe leaders on the basics of Scout leadership and how to

run outdoor programs for youth. The weekend started with Friday afternoon arrival followed by two nights of camping, sharing a tent with a
total stranger, and participating in a mocked-up patrol structure format.

When I arrived, I was randomly paired up with another adult male
participant with whom I would closely share the next couple of days
sleeping, preparing meals, practicing first aid, building fires, and pitching
tents. He was a married man with two sons who were involved in scouting. He'd just moved to Kentucky from New York State. He talked a lot
about his wife and children, and the whole time I had to speak back in
riddles because I too was married, but to another man. I suspected that
revelation would be too controversial to mention under the circumstances.

The first morning when I woke up after sharing a tent with this gen-
tleman, he informed me that I had talked a lot in my sleep during the
night. I didn't ask him what I had said because I honestly didn't want to
know if I had outed myself by sleep-talking. Don't ask, don't tell, right?
Somehow, I made it through that weekend, and the rest of my leader
training was awarded by my coveted Trained Leader patch from the BSA.
I could finally put on my official Scout uniform.

After completing some additional BSA leader training, I took over
as leader of Isaiah's den as they crossed over from Cub to the Webelos
rank. Webelos Scouts are for youth in fourth and fifth grade and who are
typically age nine to ten. In those days, Webelos Scouts spent two years
in transition to becoming Boy Scouts in the spring after turning eleven.
Webelos are usually required to do more camping and shift their focus
to outdoor activities. Cub Scouts are younger and not able or willing to
participate in physically challenging outdoor programs.

The other big difference is that at the Webelos Scout level, parents
are no longer required to stay for every den or pack meeting or attend
every activity. Parents are always welcome and encouraged to stay, and
often they do. But as long as two-deep leadership is maintained, it's ac-
ceptable for parents to drop their boys off and then return when the
scheduled activity is over. The important thing was that the parents of
the Scouts in my den trusted me to take care of their sons for meetings,
outings, and various other scouting activities.

At first I was leery about the possibility that parents would object to
having a gay Scout leader. But because I had already been active with the
den and nearly all of the Scout families had known Michael and me for
years, no one raised any concerns. In fact, more often I received great

gratitude and relief from the parents that someone—anyone—was willing to take over this time-consuming and demanding role for the den.

The first overnight outing I planned was taking our Webelos Scouts to summer camp at the Tunnel Mill Scout Reservation in Charlestown, Indiana. This involved three nights of camping. I had to recruit adults to stay with me and camp with their sons so that we could maintain two-deep leadership. That was a hard sell for these parents, but I arranged to tag-team and have one different parent stay for each of the three nights. I have always been pretty adept at organizing things, but being a Cub Scout leader really required me to focus and expand these skills into leading both adults and youth.

That particular summer camp had its challenges, notably heavy thunderstorms. We had to evacuate into the camp dining hall in the middle of the night for two consecutive nights to shelter during tornado watches. We also faced torrential rains that ended up soaking our tents, some sleeping bags, and lots of our gear. It was one of the most weather-volatile camping trips I ever took with the Scouts but also one of the most fun and most rewarding. We endured. We overcame. After those Scouts and I finished that stint, we were all confident in our ability to handle pretty much anything that Mother Nature and the scouting program might throw at us.

My role as Scout leader became increasingly comfortable, so my focus turned to getting my Webelos ready to cross over to the Boy Scout troop at Lourdes. The highest level of achievement in Cub/Webelos scouting is the Arrow of Light. My goal was to get all of my boys to that level before they became Boy Scouts. That designation required earning a series of badges and meeting other requirements, but by March 2009 when my Webelos crossed over to the Boy Scout troop, all six of my survivors had completed their Arrow of Light.

10

CROSSING OVER
TO BOY SCOUTS

My intention as I shepherded the boys through Webelos was that when they got to the Boy Scout troop I would simply back away and let the "professional" Scouts take over. I imagined these Boy Scout leaders were vastly more knowledgeable and equipped to assist the boys as they moved into and through the levels of Boy Scouting. As we got close to that point of handoff, my Webelos started attending Boy Scout troop meetings and outings. To my surprise the Boy Scout adult leaders were itching to turn the reigns of leadership over to others. They wanted to ensure the continuity of the long-standing Lourdes Boy Scout troop, but they were adult leaders whose sons had aged-out of the scouting program. They were looking to follow their sons into scouting retirement or at least greatly scale back their involvement with the troop.

This really put me in a quandary. I never wanted to be a Scout leader in the first place, but I did so for our son, who loved everything that scouting had to offer. I wanted him to have those experiences. My plan to get the boys to age eleven and turn them over to the troop was not going to work, so I had to decide whether I could or should make the crossover to the troop with my son Isaiah and the rest of my Webelos. Although my Webelos parents were aware that I was gay, I had not spent enough time with the Boy Scout troop leaders to determine if they were aware and if that would render me unsuitable in their eyes to serve as a leader.

Proceeding cautiously, I revealed my sexual orientation to the other adult leaders. Amazingly, they expressed no concern over allowing me to join the troop as a Scout leader. Shortly after that, I completed the application to become an assistant Scoutmaster with Troop 325 and filed it with our local BSA Lincoln Heritage Council. Being a Scoutmaster for the Boy Scouts also required an additional round of mandatory leader training, including more overnight training at the Scout reservation. After I completed all this training, I secured my BSA Scoutmaster credentials just in time to take my first group of Boy Scouts to an entire week at BSA summer camp.

As we approached the first week of July 2009, it became apparent to me that those adult Scout leaders who'd been in charge of the troop had already done their years at summer camp. They were expecting me to take the troop that year. That meant I was going to be in charge of twelve boys at camp for an entire week. You could say I panicked just a little. But that panic subsided when I learned that a veteran Scout leader, Don Overton, would be with me. Don's grandson Jake was going to be at camp with us all week. Still, I had never taken a group that large anywhere for that long a period of time. It was a daunting task. In the spirit of scouting, I forged on, but there really was no other choice. The other existing Scout leaders had relinquished this responsibility, so I felt compelled to face that task and push ahead. As the Boy Scout Oath says, "on my honor I will do my best."

That first week with the Lourdes Boy Scouts at Camp Crooked Creek was a real challenge. When we arrived and checked in, I quickly realized that the scale of the event was much bigger than I expected. There were dozens of troops and hundreds of Scouts and leaders in attendance that week, and they were from states all around the region. The camp staff and Scoutmasters from the other troops all appeared to be scouting pros. I worried I'd be exposed as a novice and a fraud, or even worse—a gay Scoutmaster. I had to be constantly on guard to disguise my true identity, hoping that one of my Scouts wouldn't bring it up and have word spread to other Scouts, camp staff, or Scoutmasters. It was at this point I realized that by becoming a Scout leader I had been firmly and decisively pushed back into the closet. It made me very uncomfortable. I had to remind myself it was something I was doing for our son and for the other Scouts who were now looking to me for leadership and depending on me.

Eventually I realized I only had to play it straight when I was outside our troop and in the presence of outside Scouters or District/Council representatives. That was manageable. For the next few years, I took on more and more leadership responsibilities in our troop. I worked diligently with our Scouts, especially those from my old Cub Scout den who'd crossed over, to advance them through the Boy Scout ranks. Enlisting as a merit badge counselor for a broad range of required badges also gave me the opportunity to help my Scouts tick off many of their requirements for advancement.

During this period, I was also recruited by Ann Russo, the leader of the Girl Scout unit at Lourdes, to register as an adult leader for that unit. The Boy and Girl Scouts units at Lourdes had a long history of collaborating on activities, so it made sense for me to register as Girl Scout leader to comply with Girl Scouts of Kentuckiana rules. Serving as a Girl Scout leader was a pretty minor commitment, usually only one or two activities per month, compared to the nearly daily activities required for Boy Scout leadership.

For the next two summers of 2010 and 2011, I took on complete responsibility for getting our Scouts to and through summer camp at Camp Crooked Creek in Shepherdsville, Kentucky. Each spring, new Webelos and parents would cross over to our troop, and both new and seasoned Scouts would come and go, but Isaiah stayed the course and advanced quickly through the ranks. As we planned for summer camp 2012, Isaiah and his cohort were also getting ready to start high school. This is a difficult time for many Scouts. They can lose enthusiasm for scouting as all the other distractions of high school (girls, jobs, cars, sports, etc.) start competing for their time and interest.

The thought of spending another week in the closet at Camp Crooked Creek, fretting away about being discovered and outed, began to take its toll on me. I was really starting to question why I should go on pouring so much of my time and effort into being a BSA leader when I knew that the organization would not want me there if the truth was widely known about my sexual orientation. My concern grew about the BSA policy prohibiting membership for all "known or avowed homosexuals." I became keenly fixated on it and started to take great offense. Why should there be such a policy? Had I not already proven that a gay person can be an effective adult leader? What was the defense for such a policy that all people in this category should be automatically banned without considering their abilities, wishes, or rights to be full participants in a program?

11

SUFFOCATING IN
THE SCOUT CLOSET

As I dwelled upon the thought of having to go back into the closet again for a week at summer camp, I started to feel the closet walls close in on me. Why would an organization ban me from membership simply because of my God-given sexual orientation? Hadn't it noticed my track record as a proven Scout leader? My discontent mounted.

On June 22, 2012, just about three weeks before I was supposed to take the troop to summer camp, I sat down at my laptop and wrote a letter to Barry Oxley, the Scout executive of the Lincoln Heritage Council (LHC). I openly admitted I was gay and sought guidance on the LHC's position regarding this issue. By then some Scout councils, particularly in the northeastern United States, had announced they were not enforcing the adult leader ban. In my letter I explained I had been fully trained and vetted and had been successfully leading a unit for many years. The last two paragraphs read:

> June is celebrated as Pride Month, and for the last couple of weeks I have been involved in volunteer activities at Humana and in the community to commemorate this annual event. With all that openness fresh in mind, I am finding it increasingly difficult to keep a low profile and stay "in the closet" with the Boy Scouts.
>
> So, bottom line here, I need to know where you stand on having an openly gay person serving as an adult leader in your Council. I

am not trying to cause a scene, make a statement, or looking for a media event. I just want to know if I am welcome or not. If you would prefer that I resign quietly and disappear I am perfectly ready and willing to discretely fade away if that is the best interest of the Council. If you please, just provide some direction on my best course of action.

After I printed it out, I read it a few times, then sealed it in an envelope. But I still had to ask myself, "Is this something I really want to do?" As I was walking away from my desk, I remember stopping at the top of the stairs with my letter in hand and starting to pray, asking God what I should do. Was this the right course of action for me? At that moment I received a response that clearly communicated to me: *We can do this.* I did not question where that came from. It was not a booming voice that shook the walls. There was no burning bush. But I knew at that point that God was with me and was going to be there to assist me through this trial. From there I walked right to the mail box, dropped that letter in, and then went back to planning for summer camp.

Just a few days later I received a one-line email from Oxley. It simply stated we should get together to discuss. I replied right back and tried to negotiate a meeting date, but his schedule had him traveling frequently and he was mostly unavailable. Finally, I realized, as he did every year, he'd be at the Leader Appreciation Breakfast at summer camp while I was there with my troop. So I suggested we meet after his breakfast speech to the leaders. His reply was terse, "I will be at CCC that day." He was not communicating much, but I thought to myself, thank goodness I'll finally get some resolution on this.

Troop 325 checked into Camp Crooked Creek on Sunday, July 8. The boys and I were well received by the staff during the intake process. The troop settled in our camp and unpacked into our tents. We attended the opening night campfire and ceremonies with hundreds of other campers and adults. I was feeling a little insecure about what might have happened at the LHC, but I remember crawling into my sleeping bag that night, grateful that it appeared there'd be no trouble at camp.

The next night, things took a surprising turn. In the evening after dinner, two of our Lourdes Troop 325 adult leaders arrived out of nowhere at our campsite. I had known and scouted with Tony Taylor and Dan Carter, both Troop 325 committee leaders, for several years. There was no cell phone coverage at camp, so they could not contact me in advance about their visit.

When I saw them, my first thought was they were making a surprise visit to bring the boys popsicles or some other treats, as was the custom for leaders with our troop. But no, their visit had another purpose. Tony and Dan explained to me that the LHC had been in contact with them about my letter. The LHC wanted me to resign. Dan and Tony assured me that was not their preference, that they supported me as a troop leader. They told me I was to meet there at camp the next morning with Mac Barr, the commissioner at the LHC.

That evening after I crawled into my sleeping bag, it felt quite different from the night before: I now was filled with angst about what might be waiting for me the next morning.

At 5 a.m. I arose to shave and shower before the boys got up, just like every other morning I spent at camp with them. Then after getting the boys up, through morning meal, and off for their day of merit badge work and other sessions throughout the camp, it was time for me to meet with Mac Barr. That long climb up the hill to the camp dining hall was particularly difficult that day as I worried about what I would be facing. When I entered, I noticed that, suspiciously, there were no other Scouts or staffers around. Usually there is always some kind of activity going on in that space, but on this morning, it was just Mac and I.

Mac struck me as a kind man with a gentle face but a strong handshake. Since he had asked for the meeting, I decided it was best to let him do the talking or at least to start. He explained that the Lincoln Heritage Council had received my letter and he was there to speak with me about that on their behalf. As Council commissioner, Mac was one of the "key three" leaders at the LHC. Although he never said it, he implied he'd been dispatched by Barry Oxley to deal with this situation. He was sympathetic and spoke favorably of the general cultural trend toward greater LGBTQ acceptance and inclusion in American society. The way he started out, I thought things were going to go well for me. But then things went sour. He said that the Lincoln Heritage Council wanted me to resign from my position as assistant Scoutmaster at Troop 325. He wanted me to do it right there on the spot and leave camp.

It was a stunning request. I was at a loss for words. After regaining composure, I explained to him our unit had only two leaders present in camp for the week. There was no way I could leave camp because we would not be able to maintain two-deep leadership. Only the Reverend Don Overton was with me in camp to provide adult leadership for that entire week.

At that point I started to get angry. I told him there was no way I was going to leave and abandon my troop like that or force them to pack up and go home and miss out on the rest of the week. We both cooled a bit as we talked. We finally agreed I could finish out the week with our troop, but he wanted me to resign right after camp was over. I told him I would consider it. I wasn't ready to commit to that outcome, but I would pray on it. We shook hands and went our separate ways. I was upset, confused, and honestly didn't know what to do next, so I just went back to camp and focused on making sure the boys had the best camp experience possible.

Next morning was the Leader Appreciation Breakfast. It was held each Wednesday at camp for those Scout leaders spending the entire week at camp. Each year it included a program of speakers and a speech by the Lincoln Heritage Council's Scout executive, who in this case was Barry Oxley. I knew he was going to be there based on my previous email correspondence with him, so I planned to approach him after the breakfast and discuss my situation further to make my case. But as he was speaking, Oxley apologized that he had to leave early before the program completed to attend another Scout function, so I never got my one-on-one with Barry that day.

The rest of the week was pretty routine. There were no other discussions about my matter with staff, Scouts, or leaders. Spending the week at camp always helped me rekindle my love for scouting. By the time I got home at the end of the week, I'd convinced myself not to resign without a fight. I felt like I had been strong-armed. I wanted to engage in a discussion, but I felt like an ultimatum had been issued to leave or be removed.

As I unpacked my camping gear back home, I resolved not to just give in and walk away. On July 17, 2012, I let Mac Barr know where I stood on the issue. In an email to him that day, I let him know I was not prepared to resign my position at that time. After that, things just got very quiet. I received no response or other communication from the Lincoln Heritage Council about my status.

12

OUSTED

A few weeks later, I was at work downtown. About 4 p.m., I received a call from my pastor, Father Scott Wimsett, asking me to please stop by his office on my way home from work for a brief meeting. He sounded disturbed and said he really needed to speak with me.

I will never forget that fifteen-minute drive I made from downtown Louisville to the Lourdes parking lot, which was just two blocks from our home. My mind went wild. I started wondering if the fiends at the LHC had trumped up child abuse charges against me. What if they had fabricated some other lie to discredit me just to force me out? At that time it was unclear what the organization was fully capable of doing to achieve its goals.

After pulling into the parking lot outside the parish center, I just sat in my car for a few minutes. My hands were shaking as I imagined what I might have to deal with when I went in. I momentarily thought about driving away just to avoid the meeting.

Finally, I realized I had to go face whatever it was that was waiting for me inside that parish center. When I went inside about 4:30 p.m., Father Scott greeted me warmly. He immediately put many of my fears to rest. He invited me into his office and closed the door, and we sat down to talk. Although I had been a member at Lourdes for about twenty-five years at that point, this was the first time I'd ever been called to the pastor's office. It was a comfortable place with many pictures and personal touches that made visitors feel relaxed. We settled down at the small conference table and began our discussion.

Father Scott told me how he had received an unexpected visit from two representatives from the LHC. Before then, Father Scott had no knowledge of this situation. These men, he said, had forcefully insisted that he have me removed from troop leadership.

Father Scott knew my family quite well. Our children attended the parish school, and we were regulars at Mass. He spoke up to the two LHC reps and said he did not agree it was necessary. He explained to them that my leadership was not a problem for the parish. That didn't seem to matter. They gave him two options: I could resign, or Father Scott might reluctantly be forced to remove me from leadership. Neither option was very appealing to me. But he explained if neither happened and I remained in place, the Lourdes charter with the Boy Scouts would be revoked.

After the LHC staffers left, Father Scott said he had sought and received guidance from the Archdiocese of Louisville about what his options might be to resolve the current situation. The Archdiocese informed him that under the terms of Lourdes's charter with the Boy Scouts, the parish would have to dismiss me from my position for violating BSA policy.

Father Scott is a kind and compassionate man. He made sure I knew that the parish stood behind me as a leader. But I simply could not see forcing him to have to take the unsavory action of forcing me out, nor did I want to encourage him to consider refusing to take the action and put the Lourdes Scout charter at risk of revocation. Things being what they were, I told him I'd agree to resign.

Since my departure from scouting, I have described this separation as having been "forced to resign." That seems to capture the transaction appropriately.

Soon after that, I was finally able to meet for coffee with Barry Oxley, Scout executive at the LHC, to discuss the situation. Barry was clearly a kind and Christian man. We both expressed our love and respect for the scouting program. We also discovered we shared a lot in common. I told him about my meeting with Father Scott and assured him I would resign. Barry was pleased and said I would be welcome to continue to participate in troop activities like any other parent of a Scout would be. He also welcomed a continued dialogue with me on the issue of having gay people serving as Scout leaders in the future. We concluded our meeting and left with what seemed to be mutual respect for one another.

On August 16, 2012, I typed up and mailed a letter to Barry:

Please accept my resignation as Assistant Scoutmaster at Troop 325.

Given the circumstances, I do not want to put my Pastor or my Sponsoring Organization in the unpleasant situation of having to remove me against their will from this position. I feel it is in the best interest of all concerned parties that I respectfully resign at this time.

It has been my pleasure to have been of service over the years to the youth of Cub Scout Pack 325, Boy Scout Troop 325, the Lincoln Heritage Council, and the Boy Scouts of America. I hope that I have made a positive contribution to each of these groups as that was always my intent.

So that was that. I had been forced to resign. All this transpired quietly so only a small handful of people in the Troop 325 committee and at the LHC were aware of the backstory or the ultimate outcome. It played out quietly, forcefully behind closed doors, in a Scout dining hall, a pastor's office, and in a coffee shop. The LHC got what it insisted upon while avoiding the unfavorable PR that it deserved for its heavy-handed tactics in enforcing its indefensible policy of discrimination. Those people who stood by me and took up for me had been bullied into enforcing a policy with which my friends and fellow scouters did not agree. I felt violated and compromised.

Admittedly at first, I felt some relief over having the issue resolved and behind me. But as time passed and I reflected on the episode, it really got me agitated. My pastor and troop leadership had been strongarmed into forcing me out of service. These tactics were not consistent with such stated BSA values as loyalty, inclusion, respect, and treating people fairly. The Lincoln Heritage Council's behavior struck me as hypocritical and inconsistent with what the mission of that organization was supposed to be.

The Lincoln Heritage Council and the BSA had the legal right to do this. The U.S. Supreme Court had decided in 2000 in favor of the organization in *Boy Scouts of America v. Dale*, which allowed private organizations to discriminate with their membership policies. But think about the outrage the BSA would have faced if it had used the same tactics to oust an African American leader, an Asian leader, a female leader, a Muslim leader, or pick whatever you want. Protection from discrimination on innate characteristics or religious beliefs is something that all Americans should expect and be guaranteed. This is particularly so for an organization like the BSA, which so steadfastly promotes patriotism and core American values.

After some time passed, these thoughts played over and over in my head. I reached a point where I felt people should be aware of how the BSA organization was enforcing this policy and the tactics they were using. So I contacted our local newspaper, the *Courier-Journal*, to see if they had an interest in telling the story. One of the paper's preeminent reporters, Andy Wolfson, met with me over lunch to talk about the details.

On Monday, August 20, 2012, I went to retrieve the newspaper off the front porch. There on the front page was my picture. I was in my full Scout uniform. I had a sinking feeling and thought, what have I done? The article was very supportive. It portrayed me as the victim that I was. It contained numerous glowing testimonies from parents of Scouts in our troop.

Its publication marked the launch of my public advocacy for equality and LGBTQ inclusion in scouting. Since the *Courier-Journal* was part of the Gannett group of newspapers, the article got picked up and published in a variety of publications across the country. Soon my expulsion became part of the growing trend of gay Scouts and lesbian and gay Scout leaders being forced out of BSA membership that year.

Almost immediately after the article was published, I heard via Facebook Messenger from Chris Hartman, executive director of the Fairness Campaign, Louisville's LGBTQ advocacy group. Chris offered his support and wanted to let me know he was working with his board on what moves they might take to support me. He also complemented me on doing a splendid job of getting my story out in a way that portrayed me as a blatant victim of antigay discrimination.

To further raise awareness about my treatment, a week later I launched an online petition on Change.org urging the LHC to reject the BSA's antigay policy and reinstate my membership. When the petition grew to thousands of signatures and started to gain a considerable amount of attention, Mark Anthony Dingbaum from Change.org contacted me. He wanted to work with me to promote my petition. Mark Anthony explained he'd been working with Jen Tyrrell on her wildly popular online petition after she was expelled because she's a lesbian. She'd been serving as a Cub Scout leader for her son. Change.org blasted my petition out to its followers and also sent out press releases.

A couple of weeks later, Mark Anthony connected me with Rich Ferraro, Allison Palmer, and Seth Adam at GLAAD (formerly the Gay and Lesbian Alliance Against Defamation). The momentum really started picking up steam. Change.org and GLAAD had been coordinating efforts to raise awareness about widespread discrimination within BSA. They were working closely with a newly formed organization called Scouts for Equality that was seeking to eradicate sexual orientation discrimination in scouting. Scouts for Equality was founded by Zach Wahls, a straight Eagle Scout raised by lesbian mothers. He was adamant about achieving equality and inclusion for everyone in scouting. A few years earlier, in 2011, nineteen-year-old Zach had made a famous speech about his family while arguing in favor of same-sex marriage before the Iowa House of Representatives. The YouTube video of that speech went viral and accumulated millions of views. It gave Zach a platform on which to build his organization.

Shortly after my petition ran its course, another riveting antigay discrimination case emerged. Karen Andresen launched a petition on Change.org regarding her son Ryan, who'd been denied his Eagle Award after completing all requirements simply because he came out as gay. It was a passionate plea by a distraught mother defending her teenage son from insensitive and harsh discrimination. Karen's message resounded with many. Her petition gained more than 400,000 signatures. Her campaign ultimately led Ryan to an appearance on the *Ellen DeGeneres Show* to discuss his treatment. The whole debate over the unfairness of the BSA membership policy was reaching a fevered pitch. The whole country, the media, and popular opinion appeared to be rapidly turning against the BSA.

In late September 2012, I also started efforts to reach out to Barry Oxley at the LHC to try to convince him that his council did not necessarily have to follow national policy. Mostly he seemed to avoid my calls and emails. When I finally got a response about a meeting, he did not want Chris Hartman to join us. Barry suggested we meet on October 3 at a quiet local coffee shop in my neighborhood.

It was a cordial meeting for sure. Oxley presented himself as a genuinely concerned Christian man who believed that God created all people equal. He expressed his belief that the BSA would change, but it was not yet time. It was a decision that had to be made at the national level. I left that meeting feeling grateful for his time and consideration and with new respect for him.

Although I'd been forced to resign as an adult leader, I continued to work with the Scout troop at my parish in nearly the same capacity as before my ouster. Adult leader membership was not required to serve as a merit badge counselor, plan and execute weekend camping trips, and organize service projects. There was a wide range of other scouting activities available that I could lead. So I just kept right on doing all of these things. As the parent of a Scout, I was allowed to participate and lead troop activities without actually being registered anymore as an adult leader. It was a little awkward at first because I had to take off my official Scout uniform for all scouting activities. The boys had been used to seeing me in uniform for most troop activities. Of course, I remained vigilant about following BSA's policies on two-deep leadership and no one-on-one contact to protect both the boys and myself.

Our son, Isaiah, was moving along in the BSA ranks. By January 2013, he was deep into his Eagle Scout Service Project. Although not a registered leader, I was able to work closely with him as his project coach and make sure he was making progress. At the same time, I continued to get requests from the local media to talk about the BSA policy of discrimination and my harsh treatment by the local LHC.

13

LIVE UNITED

Having had time to reflect on the discriminatory treatment received from the LHC, I began thinking about how to engage in other initiatives to put pressure on the Lincoln Heritage Council to consider changing its policy.

It occurred to me that LHC received an enormous amount of financial support from Metro United Way (MUW) in Louisville. As it happened, Michael and I were longtime donors to that organization through our employers. We were also members of the MUW Tocqueville Society of major donors. In that capacity we attended monthly luncheons with the Tocqueville Society and participated in presentations by senior MUW staff.

Moving forward with an idea, I reached out to Joe Tolan, MUW's president. I explained that MUW should reconsider whether to fund an organization that was actively participating in antigay discrimination and whether that was inconsistent with MUW's policies and values. MUW had its own policy of nondiscrimination that protected its LGBTQ employees. It prided itself on being steadfastly dedicated to diversity and inclusion.

Joe agreed with my request to meet and asked his board chair, Joe Brown, and Chris Hartman from the Fairness Campaign to join the discussion. We arranged to meet on October 8, 2012, at MUW offices in downtown Louisville.

Prior to that meeting, I had not met Chris Hartman in person. After signing in at the MUW lobby, I approached him and stuck out my hand to shake his. Instead he threw his arms open and hugged me. He told me he doesn't shake hands, preferring to hug people instead. It threw me off a bit, but from that point on I knew to expect that with Chris.

When we were taken to the meeting room, Joe Tolan and Joe Brown greeted us. We had a cordial discussion. They expressed concern and regret over the way I'd been mistreated by the LHC. The BSA had been a problem for the MUW for years, they said, because its discriminatory policy was well known. Many people would not donate to the MUW or did so grudgingly, knowing that tens of thousands of dollars each year went to support the LHC. Joe Tolan confirmed his organization did not believe in or tolerate discrimination. On the other hand, they could not set policy for their member organizations.

We had an in-depth discussion about how detrimental discrimination can be for LGBTQ youth and how homelessness and suicide were epidemic in the community because of it. We left with assurances that MUW would evaluate its funding of the LHC, but they made no promises or guarantees. We felt our concerns had been heard and were genuinely being taken under consideration.

A few weeks passed and I went back to concentrating on my day job, my family, and my Scouts. In early November I received a message from Chris saying he wanted to get together and talk about the next steps with the MUW. Since I worked downtown, we met on a workday at a convenient restaurant and had a long lunch where we got to know each other in person. We began to strategize about how we could collaborate to convince the LHC and BSA to change their discriminatory policies. The best way to approach the issue, we believed, was to continue to pressure sources of financial support for the LHC, our local Scout council.

It was enlightening to get to know Chris. Louisville being what it is, we quickly found out we had much in common. We both attended Saint Stephen Martyr Elementary School and Saint Xavier High School, but I was at least a generation older than he. Little did we realize in those early days of our collaboration just how much work we would do together over the following years on a wide range of LGBTQ efforts in our city, state, and throughout the country.

14

SCOUTS IN PROTEST

In January 2013, Mark Anthony Dingbaum contacted me again. He said that GLAAD and Change.org were planning a coordinated petition delivery to BSA headquarters in Irving, Texas, just outside Dallas, in advance of the upcoming national BSA convention in Grapevine, another Dallas suburb. They were going to deliver more than 1.2 million signatures from several Change.org petitions that were calling for an end to antigay discrimination in the BSA. The plan involved having several of the people who started those petitions to deliver four large cardboard boxes containing petition signatures. Also participating in the petition delivery would be representatives from Change.org and GLAAD, and both organizations wanted the whole Bourke De Leon family to participate.

They were scheduling the petition delivery for Monday, February 4, just outside BSA national headquarters. We heard the BSA Board of Directors was going to be in a closed-door session that might include a vote on changing the policy. We were hopeful that our media event would help sway the board.

On that day, in addition to our family we were joined by Change .org petitioners Jennifer Tyrrell; Ryan Andresen's father, Eric; and Will Oliver. Will was an openly gay young man and Eagle Scout who petitioned the National Geographic Channel to denounce the Boy Scouts' antigay policy before airing its new TV series *Are You Tougher Than a Boy Scout?* The four of us were joined by our ground support team, which included Seth Adam from GLAAD, Mark Anthony Dingbaum from Change.org, and Brad Hankins, a cofounder of Scouts for Equality.

The event at BSA HQ presented me an opportunity to speak before a large number of media. The GLAAD and Change.org people were masterful at getting the media excited about events like this. Isaiah and I wore our official Boy Scout uniforms, as did Will Oliver, Jen Tyrrell, and Brad Hankins. Each of the petitioners took turns addressing the media with our stories of discrimination. Having prepared some notes, I nervously read those to the camera, but before I started I prefaced my statement with a prayer calling for God's intervention in eliminating antigay discrimination from scouting. Some of the media and others in attendance reacted with a little surprise, but anyone in scouting knows that prayer and reverence are staples of scouting activities. It seemed the appropriate way to begin, even if others didn't think so.

After we finished speaking, we answered questions and took photos for both the media and for use by GLAAD and Change.org. No one from BSA headquarters engaged with us or offered to officially meet with us. We were not allowed to actually take the petitions up to the building but had to leave them with a security team just outside.

To celebrate what felt like a very successful day, we all went out to dinner and shared our sense of accomplishment. That allowed my family the opportunity to get to know and connect with fellow petitioners Jen Tyrrell, Eric Andresen, and Will Oliver in a way that we had not been able to do previously before meeting in person. From that point on I considered them great friends and allies in the growing movement to bring equality to scouting. We ended up collaborating frequently over the coming months and years. It also gave me the chance to develop deeper working relationships with Mark Anthony Dingbaum, Seth Adam, and Brad Hankins. They all proved to be great personal supporters and allies in the evolving Scouts for Equality movement.

After our family returned to Louisville, on Wednesday, February 6, 2013, the BSA issued a press release stating it had delayed a vote on its policy banning gay youth and leaders. From that point on, speculation was that BSA would take up the issue at its annual convention in Grapevine, Texas, in May. The lobbying on both sides of the issue intensified.

The second weekend of February each year, our parish celebrates the Feast of Our Lady of Lourdes and has an annual Lourdes Night dinner and program. This is an event that Michael and I attend every year. But for 2013, I was surprised to have been nominated for and won a Stewardship Award for my service to the Lourdes community. It was a great surprise to me because these awards typically go to people who are long-standing volunteers at the parish. Apparently I'd earned that designation after many years of volunteering with many different ministries. Honestly, I think it was likely a sympathy award because of the way I had been mistreated by the BSA and LHC.

After our February petition delivery, I continued communicating with Mark Anthony at Change.org, Seth Adam at GLAAD, and Zach Wahls, founder of Scouts for Equality. The focus of our conversations was my efforts at convincing Louisville's Metro United Way to drop its substantial funding of the LHC. Chris Hartman and I had been pressuring MUW to defund LHC because, although the group did have language protecting its own employees from antigay discrimination, it financially supported the BSA LHC as one of its top annual beneficiaries from grant awards. Since Michael and I were members of MUW's Tocqueville Society for major donors, we could not be easily ignored by MUW staff and administration. But it was clear MUW was playing both sides of the fence. It was not willing yet in early 2013 to take a bold stand supporting LGBTQ equality for fear of alienating the part of its donor base who thought that discrimination was actually justified.

After some back and forth with Mark Anthony and Zach Wahls, we decided I should launch another Change.org petition calling for the MUW to denounce the BSA for its discriminatory member policies. Just a couple of days after we returned from the event at BSA headquarters, I was taking our Boy Scout troop on a cave camping trip. While I was gone, the folks at GLAAD, Change.org, and Scouts for Equality team were busy crafting the right message for a petition.

On February 11, my new petition officially launched. As word spread, it quickly generated more than 60,000 signatures. This was part of a larger strategy by Scouts for Equality and its partners to start challenging other organizations that financially supported BSA. It targeted corporate entities such as Intel, Verizon, and UPS because they had progressive policies protecting and supporting their LGBTQ employees but also provided substantial financial support to the BSA.

That same week, something really extraordinary happened. Isaiah fully completed his Eagle Scout Service Project. He did this by leading a team of volunteers that installed eight bat houses in Iroquois Park, one of Louisville's treasured Olmsted parks. I was personally so proud of him for getting that Eagle Project done and staying focused on his advancement despite all the publicity and discussion that was swirling around me and my battles with the BSA.

After my United Way petition grew, it came to my attention that the United Way Worldwide was having its national convention in nearby Indianapolis. Working with Mark Anthony Dingbaum, we decided it would be worth it to stage another petition delivery at the national convention.

From a distance, Mark Anthony at Change.org and Zach Wahls at Scouts for Equality were providing support, but when it came time to make the delivery on April 17, 2013, it was just me in my car with the petition box and no ground support. When I arrived in Indianapolis, I met up with a group of local television and newspaper reporters and held a press conference. Prior to that day I'd been in correspondence with Keri Albright, president of the Susquehanna Valley United Way in Pennsylvania. She was a great supporter of my efforts to reform scouting. Keri met me at the press conference and stuck with me through much of the day. It was a great relief to have such personal support since the other national organizations could not have been there.

It was a little hectic, but I managed to pull off the interviews and arranged a meeting with United Way Worldwide president Stacey Stewart and Joe Tolan, president of the MUW of Louisville, who was attending the convention. I caused quite a stir among convention goers as I walked through the convention center in my Scout uniform with several reporters and news cameras flanking me. In my arms was a large box with the petition signatures and a sign on the box touting the number of signatures. It urged the United Way to stop funding BSA until it halted its antigay discrimination. When I met with Stewart and Tolan, they could not have been more sympathetic and encouraging to me in my efforts. After that, the movement to challenge financial supporters of BSA continued to gain steam.

15

INCLUSIVE
SCOUTING SUMMIT

On May 6, 2013, Mark Noel, one of the founders of the Inclusive Scouting Network, informed me that a counter meeting was being planned at the Great Wolf Lodge across the street from BSA's national convention in Grapevine, Texas. Called the Equal Scouting Summit, it would be taking place simultaneously with the national convention. They had invited participants in the BSA meeting to visit and hear their arguments for inclusive scouting.

When the meeting convened, in attendance were a large group from Scouts for Equality, including founders Zach Wahls and Brad Hankins, plus other prominent of its leaders, such as Justin Bickford, Justin Wilson, Kate Searle, and Ken Schulz. The Inclusive Scouting Network organization sent Mark Noel, Dave Knapp, Dave Rice, and Matt Comer. Also in attendance were supporters Dave McGrath and his adult son, Joe, who were making a long-distance bike ride from Idaho to Dallas to raise awareness with the media about the upcoming summit and BSA vote.

Several petitioners who had experienced BSA discrimination were also recruited to attend and retell their stories, including Jen Tyrrell, Will Oliver, and I. A new petitioner also joined, young Pascal Tessier and his mother, Tracie Felker. Pascal was just seventeen, openly gay, and seeking to change the youth membership policy, even though he had not yet been a victim of discrimination from his progressive Maryland Boy Scout troop. Attending from the national organizations we also had Seth Adam and Allison Palmer from GLAAD and Mark Anthony Dingbaum from Change.org. The summit started on Wednesday, May 22, 2013, and ran through Friday, May 24. Since our kids had already missed some school in February to attend the BSA petition delivery, Michael and I decided it was best for me to attend alone without the rest of our family.

On the morning of Wednesday, May 22, I flew to Dallas and barely made it in time for the noon press conference to kick off the summit. It was a short but frantic drive from the airport to the conference facility. I remember arriving shortly before the event in my rental car with no time to spare, only to find a distant and vacant part of the parking lot where I could swiftly change into my Class A Boy Scout uniform. After a sprint through the Great Wolf Lodge to find the conference center, I got there just in the nick of time before the press conference began.

As usual I had notes prepared to address the media, but I wasn't prepared to have to follow Zach Wahls with my speech. Zach is an incredibly persuasive orator who can sell just about anything to anyone, as he proved in that YouTube video. He was the last person I wanted to follow, but after Zach adeptly kicked things off, it was my turn to tell my discrimination story. All the other petitioners after me made solid cases for eliminating BSA's discrimination policies immediately.

After we finished speaking and answering questions from the media, we all hung around the rest of the afternoon. We entertained sporadic visitors from the media and official Scouters who came over from the BSA convention across the street to show support for the Inclusive Scouting Summit. As the day came to a close, Mark Anthony organized what he called a *family dinner* that included most of the summit participants. We shared a satisfying meal, talked about the successes of the day, and speculated on the good news we hoped would come from the BSA meeting across the street in the next day or two.

Early the next morning, summit attendees gathered again at our conference space at the Great Wolf Lodge and we settled into our "war room" to monitor the progress of the discussions at the BSA convention. Brad Hankins took the lead in monitoring message boards and other online sources to look for hints about if and when a decision would be made. Zach Wahls handled an endless stream of media requests to answer questions about the summit and the BSA meeting. The BSA was expected to take the vote at any time that day, so no one wanted to leave the area and take the chance of missing the announcement.

In late afternoon, after a tense day of waiting, we got word that the BSA had voted to officially change its youth policy to allow gay youth members. It had passed a favorable membership resolution with more than 60 percent of the vote.

The Inclusive Scouting Summit war room erupted in celebration. There was an incredible feeling of success and relief with the outcome. As the news sank in and was quickly confirmed from another official source, it dawned on me that, as happy as I was for any movement whatsoever by the BSA, the policy change applied only to youth members, not adults. It did not affect my situation or that of other adult gay and lesbian leaders. We were still banned from participation.

The press made its rounds. Zach Wahls did most of the talking, but everyone expressed gratitude that the BSA had changed its youth membership policy. Many of us, including my friend Jen Tyrrell and I, got to accentuate the point that we would continue to be discriminated against because the adult membership policy had not been changed. It was a bittersweet partial victory for LGBTQ inclusion in the BSA, but it was far from a complete resolution. Representatives from Scouts for Equality and all the Equal Scouting Summit participants and supporters also vowed to keep working for full adult membership inclusion. Then we all went on our separate ways back home to regroup.

16

WINDSOR AND PROP 8

For quite some time my world had been consumed with my career, family (including my elderly parents), my scouting activities with my troop, and the efforts to reform the BSA membership policy. I simply did not take the time to pay attention to the national news or even other LGBTQ rights developments. But in late May 2013 something broke through the clutter. I started hearing a lot of media coverage about upcoming U.S. Supreme Court rulings on California's Proposition 8 and the Edie Windsor case, *United States v. Windsor*. Not knowing the details of what they were about, Michael and I both hurried to get up to speed and started paying attention as the pending decisions came closer.

On June 26, 2013, in a pair of 5 to 4 decisions the Supreme Court ruled in favor of the plaintiffs in both cases. The Prop 8 case allowed a lower court ruling to stand, saying that California could not ban same-sex marriage because it would violate its citizens' equal protection rights under the law.[1] The ruling applied only to California, but it seemed to open the door to similar challenges in other states.

The *Windsor* case was even more of an earthquake because it ruled that portions of the U.S. Defense of Marriage Act (DOMA) of 1996 were unconstitutional under the due process clause of the Fifth Amendment. Edie Windsor and her longtime partner and legal spouse from a 2007

---

1. *Hollingsworth v. Perry*, 570 U.S. 693 (2013), https://supreme.justia.com/cases/federal/us/570/693/.

Canadian marriage were denied spousal death benefits that would have been afforded an opposite-sex couple.

This double whammy by the Court in favor of same-sex marriage sent the LGBTQ community into a frenzy. It also riled conservatives who had fought long and hard against the advancement of marriage equality. But that day was a turning point because it signaled the intentions of the Supreme Court on this issue, and it seemed to invite more opportunities for change.

When the *Windsor* ruling was announced, I remember sitting in my office at Humana trolling the major newswires on the Internet.[2] After the news hit, there was great joy in cyberspace. On social media there was an announcement of an afternoon celebration rally in Louisville that was going to take place in a public park across from City Hall. It was just three blocks over from my work. I decided to saunter over at lunchtime and hang out during the rally. It was a major LGBTQ party that celebrated perhaps the two greatest victories to date in our quest for equality. There was much joy, many hugs, and much enthusiasm as Chris Hartman of the Fairness Campaign led the crowd through many chants and cheers. After returning to my office, I thought, okay, that's over. Now let's just move on to other things.

Looming ahead was my plan to take the Lourdes Troop 325 to yet another week of summer camp at Crooked Creek from July 7 to July 13. You can't imagine how much planning goes into getting a dozen or more preteen boys ready for a week in the woods. It was a week constantly busy with advancement activities but also lots of fun. Even though I was no longer a registered adult leader, I served as informal leader at camp a couple more years after my ousting.

The Scout families all trusted me. I had completed all the necessary training. I was a veteran leader. So it just made sense for me to carry on. We followed the principles of two-deep leadership and no one-on-one contact strictly by making sure we had plenty of other adult supervision at Scout camp. By 2013, I had grown particularly bold at summer camp, wearing my Scouts for Equality T-shirts and my Inclusive Scouting Network insignia. These symbols generated numerous very kind and supportive comments from camp staff.

---

2. *United States v. Windsor*, 570 U.S. 744 (2013), https://supreme.justia.com/cases/federal/us/570/744/.

17

BOURKE V. BESHEAR

Shortly after the Prop 8 and *Windsor* decisions came down, Michael heard from Tonya Miller, a Human Resources manager where he worked at General Electric. Tonya had deep connections in the local LGBTQ community, and she had put word out among her contacts about David Corbett, a close friend. David was in contact with a couple of local lawyers who wanted to file a case in Kentucky challenging the state constitutional ban on same-sex marriage.

After a brief discussion, Michael and I decided we had too much on our plates already and it would be better to let someone else handle that quest. But as time passed, Tonya let Michael know that no one was stepping up to commit to work with the attorneys. Michael and I reluctantly decided that if no one else was going to do this, we would have to.

Before starting the ball rolling with the attorneys, we decided to talk to our children first about this. Our kids at that age were pretty typical teenagers who didn't seem to be very aware of or concerned about social issues. When we told them we were considering suing the state to recognize our marriage, they were surprised because they just assumed we were already recognized as married. After all, they were present for and participated in our legal wedding ceremony in Ontario in 2004, and so as far as they knew it was a done deal. As we talked about it, they became quite engaged and encouraged us to pursue it with their blessings.

Michael funneled the word back through his contact that we would be interested in talking to the attorneys. Tonya passed our contact information on to David, past chair of the Kentucky Fairness Alliance. She recommended us as suitable candidates for a lawsuit because of our recent exposure with the BSA campaign for equality. David then introduced us by email for the first time to attorneys Shannon Fauver and Dawn Elliott. Shannon and Dawn, both fierce straight allies, had been business partners in a two-person law practice for several years.

Dawn got back to us right away. The conversation started with us asking a few questions about fees and time commitments. We moved on to our legal arguments about how our family over the years had been harmed by not having full marriage equality. Foremost with us was not being able to jointly adopt our children, and all the uncertainty and angst that arose from that over the years. Heaven forbid, if something would have happened to Michael, upon his passing I would have had no legal relationship with or claim to custody for our children since he was the only legal parent for them. But there were also many other considerations, such as paying extra taxes because we weren't considered legally married, and not having shared access to benefits from our employers over the years the way other married couples did. Dawn and Shannon were interested, but they had a meeting scheduled with the ACLU about support for the case in a few days. After that, they would call us to discuss a game plan.

When we didn't hear right back after the ACLU meeting, I emailed Dawn about what was going on. She replied on July 5, 2013: "The bottom line of their discussion is that they don't think KY will be the first state to change the law (we already knew that) but they encouraged us to go ahead with the lawsuit. With that being said, we will press on and when it comes time to file it (July 22, 2013), we will of course email you a copy for your review. This is going to be so awesome!!! Dawn."

Several weeks passed without any contact. We were beginning to wonder if anything was going to happen. Finally, on July 21 we heard from Shannon Fauver. She asked if we wanted to include our minor children as plaintiffs. After another Bourke De Leon family meeting, our children agreed they should be included because they also had much at stake in the case. Shannon asked us to provide as many details as possible about when and where Michael and I were married and the same for how our children joined the family so they could build that part of the case. Although all of her and Dawn's services were being provided without charge, Shannon said we'd have to put up the initial filing fee.

On Thursday, July 25, an email arrived from Shannon. She was putting the final tweaks on the lawsuit, which she'd be filing the next morning at the U.S. District Court for the Western District of Kentucky. I replied immediately: "Will we get to see the lawsuit before it gets filed? Just curious about what we are getting ourselves into. Whatever it is, I'm sure it will be worth the ride." Up to that point we still had not met either of our attorneys in person. We'd been communicating only via email. Nor had we seen any written legal arguments. That was just a little cause of concern for us, but eventually we did get a view of the draft document before filing.

Shannon asked if we could meet her at the Federal Courthouse in downtown Louisville at 9:30 a.m. the next morning, Friday July 26, 2013. Michael and I agreed. We adjusted our work schedules to allow us to be there for the filing. Before that happened, very early that morning, I received an email from a local reporter, Scott Adkins from WAVE3 News, who wanted to talk to Michael and me. I contacted Shannon, who had initiated the connection, to make sure it was okay to talk to Scott. Ultimately, we decided that Scott would meet Shannon and Michael and me at the courthouse for the filing and we could talk then.

The Federal Courthouse was a short walk from my office at the Humana Tower, so I arrived a few minutes early. Shannon was already there on the steps. She was dressed in a dark business suit that accentuated by contrast her beautiful long red hair. Scott Adkins was also already there and was setting up for interviews. Shannon explained that we really didn't have to physically file any paperwork because that was all done electronically, so our appearance at the courthouse was just symbolic. Shannon and Scott wanted to get started, but I put them off until Michael arrived. He was delayed because he got his wires crossed and went to the Jefferson County Courthouse instead of the Federal Courthouse, so he had to rush to join us and walked briskly for several blocks in the summer heat to get there.

After our interview with Scott was over, Shannon's phone started blowing up with requests from other media. She quickly improvised and invited them to an unscheduled press conference at her office on Frankfort Avenue a couple of miles from the courthouse. Michael and I had not planned on taking that much time off from work. We thought a half hour at the courthouse for filing would do, and then we could go on about our workday. As it turned out, neither of us went back to work that day. When we got to Shannon's office, reporters were arriving from all over town. We got busy moving around furniture in the conference room to accommodate all the interest. We talked to reporters for what seemed like hours. In addition, national media was calling from all over wanting to talk to the attorneys, Michael, and me. It was a remarkable, surprising, and exhausting day that we certainly had not anticipated.

That afternoon we also met Dawn Elliott for the first time in person and immediately fell in love with her confident and irreverent style. Dawn was a strong, persuasive Black attorney with great presence who believed deeply in fighting for equality for all people under the law. She and Shannon had gone to law school together at the University of Louisville. They made a fabulous pair of freedom fighters. Even though we'd just met them, we loved them in an instant. We also learned more about Shannon, whom I can best describe as a bit of a carryover from the 1960s social progressives with whom I'd grown up. Shannon could have been a flower child in those earlier days, but in this era she was fiercely dedicated to equality. For her, that included a length of service with the Peace Corps after college.

It was not until the hubbub of that day and under those hectic circumstances that we heard that Shannon and Dawn had been working with another couple from Shelbyville, Kim Franklin and Tammy Boyd, about filing a similar case in the U.S. District Court for the Eastern District of Kentucky. Because they lived in a county just east of ours, that case needed to be filed in Lexington. But neither Dawn nor Shannon had current credentials to do that, so their filing had been delayed, which meant ours went first. Up to that point we assumed we were the only Kentuckians interested in taking on this task. Later we met Tammy and Kim and grew to love them as fellow marriage equality advocates and plaintiffs.

On that filing date the media was intensely scrutinizing us. I remember feeling totally embarrassed because Michael was wearing his wedding ring and I was not. As we sat at the Fauver Law Office conference table addressing the cameras, I found myself covering my left hand with my right hand so people could not see I was not wearing a wedding ring. A few days earlier I'd lost it after wearing it pretty consistently for nearly nine years. In those days my fingers would swell quite a bit, so I'd slip my ring off for a while and put it in my pocket or on a nightstand to give my finger a break. The week before we filed the lawsuit, I lost it forever. I can't tell you how many times I dug through my clothes and all of the trash and recycle bins looking for that ring, but I couldn't find it. After we finished the interviews that day, I came home, made a drink, and ordered a replacement on Amazon.

Over the next few days, countless friends and strangers offered us their support. One offer came from Andy Downey, a fellow U of L alumnus. I'd been working with him to establish an LGBT Alumni Council at U of L. Andy was an attorney and board member of ACLU of Kentucky and offered to help. I asked Dawn if it would be appropriate for him to intercede with the ACLU of Kentucky to assist. Dawn replied on July 29, 2013: "We have had contact with the ACLU. If you speaking with them will somehow change their mind about getting onboard, I'm definitely down for that ;) Dawn." It was through that message, and with other conversations with our attorneys, that we learned our local ACLU was not at all "onboard" and in fact was concerned our case might do more harm than good.

That was actually a common theme at the time of filing. Pretty much no organization, local or national, thought we had much of a chance. Michael and I remember one interview we did the day of the filing with the *Huffington Post*. The reporter kept grilling us about whether the suit might do more harm than good to the cause if we lost our case. That scenario was what most people expected in conservative Kentucky. We were instructed that other national leaders in the marriage equality movement had a "roadmap to victory" and Kentucky was not on that route. Michael would later joke that we made our own on-ramp to that highway. It was more than a little disheartening to get so much criticism and lack of support, but at that point Michael and I had lived thirty-one years together thinking it was just us against the world, so we were not particularly discouraged by the lack of organizational support.

After the filing, things quieted down while our attorneys worked feverishly to refine their legal arguments. They also worked to add additional plaintiffs to our case. Dawn and Shannon were convinced the case would have more importance for the judge if there were more plaintiff stories to consider: a sort of a strength in numbers approach. Michael and I were not opposed at all to that approach. Based on their counsel, we approved adding other plaintiffs to the case.

In the interim we went back to our mundane lives of corporate jobs, parenting teenagers, caring for aging parents, parish volunteer activities, and, yes, scouting. I continued to work diligently with the troop as a quasi-leader, even though I could not register with BSA. People in our troop and in our parish disregarded the BSA expulsion and allowed me to mostly carry on with business as usual.

My biggest personal project was getting Isaiah across the finish line to Eagle rank. On August 1, 2013, he successfully completed his Eagle Board of Review. I could not have been prouder of him as a parent and Scout leader. He deserved all the credit for his ability to get that accomplished despite all of the frenzy over my scouting expulsion and then the lawsuit. Walking home from the Board of Review with Isaiah was one of those father–son moments of bonding, sharing, and love that you see occasionally in the really sentimental TV commercials.

Over the following weeks, Shannon and Dawn added two other couples to our case. One of them was Paul Campion and Randy Johnson of Louisville and their four children. We had known them for about fifteen years. Paul and Randy had been active with us as part of Rainbow Families of Kentucky, a small local group of gay and lesbian couples with children. The Johnson-Campions had adopted twin boys as infants about 1995. We'd used the same adoption agency. Randy was a medical professional with the Veterans Administration and Paul a public school counselor. We knew they had gotten legally married in California when that window was open. Like us, they were joining the case to have their legal marriage recognized.

The other couple was Luke Barlow and Jimmy Mead of Bardstown, Kentucky, who'd legally married in Iowa. They'd already been together forty-five years. In the meantime, Shannon had renewed her credentials in the Eastern District of Kentucky and was able to successfully file the lawsuit in Lexington for Kim Franklin and Tammy Boyd. Ultimately the Franklin case was moved from the Eastern District to the Western and all four couples merged together and became *Bourke v. Beshear*.

As late August approached, Michael got the notion we should get all the plaintiffs and attorneys together to meet in person and get to know one another. We offered up our home and made it a potluck gathering. We coordinated our schedules for September 8. I always shuddered when Michael wanted to have people over because with two teenagers and our busy work and volunteer schedules, we never had time to clean. Still, we knew it was important for us to get to know our fellow plaintiff families and attorneys better before we all went any further down the path of our journey together.

Paul and Randy and their family were old friends, and we thoroughly enjoyed meeting Tammy and Kim and Luke and Jim. We all got along just splendidly. After that evening, we all stayed closely connected via group email chains that allowed us to address issues and concerns. We were also able to resolve issues that came up with our attorneys pretty quickly.

Something truly unexpected hit my email box in late August. It was an inquiry from Seth Adam at GLAAD asking me if I was interested in a photo shoot for *OUT* magazine. He told me I'd been named to the annual *OUT* 100 list of the year's most compelling LGBTQ people. What??? Flyover state Kentucky was really not on the radar screen when it came to things like this. Typically those honors go to advocates on the coasts working in big cities. But *OUT* magazine had taken notice of my work with the equal scouting movement. Also to be honored were Dave Knapp and Pascal Tessier, both of whom I got to know pretty well in Texas at the Equal Scouting Summit. *OUT* decided to name all three of us to its *OUT* 100 list for 2013. What made this group of three remarkable was that Dave Knapp was in his eighties, I was in my fifties, and Pascal Tessier was just seventeen, so we represented three generations of scouts and scouters who had been discriminated against and who had been fighting for equality in the BSA.

The prospect made me a little nervous because I had not been to New York City since the 1980s, but Seth reassured me he would help with all the details. The commitment required travel to NYC in early September, so I agreed and started working through the details. Seth told me to remember to pack my Scout uniform because the photo shoot would be a joint session with the other two Scouts in their uniforms.

Early September came and I nervously boarded a flight from Louisville to New York. I took a cab to GLAAD's offices where I met up with Pascal and his mother, Tracie, and Dave Knapp. After a brief reunion, we took a car over to a photo studio in Brooklyn where we received makeup and were treated like celebrities. This was very uncomfortable for me because I was a nerdy data analyst for a health insurance company who'd never had makeup applied before in my life. The studio had a few Scout-related props we could use, and there were a lot of throwaway pictures taken with ropes and neckerchiefs. The best picture was one of the three of us in our scout uniforms saluting the camera. It remains iconic, at least to me. I've kept that as my Facebook cover photo since 2013 as a deliberate protest. I plan to leave it there indefinitely until I'm finally allowed to return as a registered leader at my parish-sponsored troop.

The photographer for that session was Danielle Levitt. I hadn't heard of her before the shoot but quickly learned she was a famous photographer and director. Danielle was charming. She was amazed to hear that my husband and I had been together for more than thirty years. That didn't happen very often in her circle of friends. There was a production line moving through her studio that day for the *OUT* 100 honorees, so we all got to mingle and share stories. A couple of the other honorees were former scouts themselves. They were thrilled to see us there and thanked us profusely for the work we were doing to change BSA's membership policy.

After I returned to Kentucky, the next few weeks were full of email discussions among the plaintiffs about all sorts of issues. The Kentucky Equality Federation organization was asking Michael and me and some of the others to join a state lawsuit they wanted to file in Kentucky's Franklin Circuit Court. But after deliberating at length with our attorneys and the other plaintiffs, we all decided it was better not to stretch ourselves any more than we already were. Attention was appropriately redirected to the federal cases.

On September 16, 2013, Shannon Fauver let the plaintiffs know that she had "just received a phone call from the Attorney General's office and they asked that we agree to allow them to respond to both lawsuits on the same day, which is the 25th, as it will be the same answer. For various reasons, I said yes, but mostly as I just told him about the Ohio cases, which he was not aware of, which as discussed aren't binding but give them an out if they want to rule as other states in our Federal Circuit are."

Kentucky attorney general Jack Conway (D) and Kentucky governor Steve Beshear (D) were both named in our federal lawsuit against the state, so we were hopeful they'd release a sympathetic response in line with what we were hearing from elected Democrats in other states across the country.

The next development was a call that Shannon received on September 25 from the Kentucky Attorney General's Office. It asked if we'd agree to consolidate the cases from the Eastern District of Kentucky and the Western District. The AG proposed combining them all in the Western District. Shannon advised it would likely be advantageous because they felt the chances of a favorable decision were better with Louisville's more progressive judges. The Kentucky plaintiff group agreed and waited patiently for the AG's response, which was expected any day.

Kentucky's AG Conway finally issued a statement on October 2. The state, it said, would defend its ban on same-sex marriage. Our assumptions, the AG stated, were incorrect in filing our lawsuit. Shannon comforted us all, saying it was the expected response. Actually, there was some good news. The AG did not make a motion to dismiss the case, which might have been successful. (As AG, Jack Conway could have motioned to have it dismissed and that would have been a powerful ask from an AG. He couldn't dismiss it himself because it was a federal and not a state case, but such a motion would have been seriously considered and might have been granted.) At least we were still in the game. We all advanced to the next round.

The case had been assigned to Judge John Heyburn, who'd been recommended in 1992 by conservative Senator Mitch McConnell (R-KY) to President George H. W. Bush for appointment to the U.S. District Court for the Western District. Those factors greatly concerned the plaintiffs, but our attorneys reassured us that Judge Heyburn had a moderate track record on rulings. A much more unfavorable judge might have been drawn in the Western District. An October 10, 2013, phone call between our attorneys and Judge Heyburn initiated the process. Afterwards, Shannon let the plaintiffs know by email that "between the judge's tone and his suggestions as to how the case should progress, we feel confident that he is receptive to our case."

The next day, another surprise arrived via email from Seth Adam at GLAAD. He told me to be on the lookout for an invitation to the *OUT* 100 Gala in New York City. As he described it, it was one of the biggest LGBTQ events of the year. I thought to myself, they must have me confused with somebody else. But a few days later the invite arrived, and Michael and I started making plans to attend the event in November. Since our kids were not yet old enough to drive themselves about, and we weren't ready to leave them alone at home for a couple of days, we asked Michael's sister Debra to fly into town and supervise our kids while we were in New York.

Before we could make the trip, October 2013 brought several important developments. Perhaps the highlight for our family was the celebration of Isaiah's Eagle Scout Court of Honor. He shared the ceremony with another one of my Scouts, Eagle honoree Geordie Ayers. After the ceremony, a reception was held in the cafeteria at Lourdes. When I was ousted in August 2012, I'd taken off my Scout leader uniform and afterwards had never worn it to Troop 325 functions. But on that night, I put it back on and wore it to the ceremony just so I could get some pictures together with Isaiah in uniform. Isaiah and I had been sharing that path to Eagle for so many years, so I wanted to be there in full uniform to show support for him as he crossed the finish line.

During the ceremony he was awarded a Scout Mentor pin, which Scouts are supposed to present to the person who influenced their success in scouting the most. Isaiah called me out and fastened his Mentor pin on my Scout uniform shirt. We shared a long embrace in front of a room full of people as we both choked back tears. All of that effort of being a supportive scout dad had finally come to fruition. It was very satisfying.

Later that month, Shannon and Dawn told us they wanted to accept an offer to receive legal assistance with the case from some prominent attorneys in town at the firm Clay Daniel Walton & Adams. Laura Landenwich and Dan Canon were well-known Louisville attorneys with experience in civil rights law. They wanted to join our case as counsel because they sensed its potential significance. Another junior attorney from the firm, Joe Dunman, would also join. These three would work with Shannon and Dawn to refine our filings, prepare arguments, manage communications with the judge, and perform a variety of other legal tasks.

Shannon and Dawn had worked pro bono on the case for several months and it was consuming their personal and professional lives. They desperately felt the need to accept this offer for assistance. The plaintiffs understood and had no concerns with adding these legal professionals to the team. The plaintiff families met on November 12 at Shannon and Dawn's office to sign affidavits and meet our new attorneys.

A few days later, I came down with a miserable cough and sore throat complete with intermittent chills and fever. I was in no condition to travel. But I persevered. Michael and I flew to New York the day before the *OUT* 100 Gala. My hope was I'd magically get better and be in fine shape before the event. That did not happen. Living on Nyquil and Day-quil, I was exhausting myself from the constant coughing that nothing could tame. Not exactly the health one hopes when attending a gala, but since we got to New York a day early I had a little time to rest and recover in the hotel room.

The next morning, I woke up feeling a little better, but that didn't last long. Once again, I loaded myself up with cold medicine and slugged through the day. I had no business going out in public, but we had made so many arrangements to get there. I didn't want to let Michael or the people at GLAAD down by not showing. When it was time, I took a long hot shower, got out my Scout uniform, neatly pressed it, and put it on precisely. Then we walked the few blocks from our hotel to the event site.

When we arrived, I quickly forgot about my illness. The excitement of the event lifted me up and carried me through the night. The *OUT* 100 Gala was held at Terminal 5 in Hell's Kitchen, which was a magnificent venue and very intimate for the few hundred people attending. While waiting in the line to go down the red carpet, we noticed Edie Windsor was right there with us in line. We walked over, made introductions, and told her we were marriage equality plaintiffs from Kentucky. Of course we hit it off splendidly. After talking a while about her case and ours, we exchanged contact information. We kept in touch with each other over the coming years.

After going through the red carpet line and having our photos taken, Michael and I went out to mingle among the crowd. The *Out* 100 that year had an all-star cast of honorees. Among them were Sir Ian McKellen, John Waters, Bruce Vilanch, Janet Mock, Roberta Kaplan, Lea DeLaria, Steve Grand, and Laverne Cox. They weren't all in attendance that night, but I kept getting whiplash from seeing all the prominent folks from the LGBTQ movement walking about.

For most of the evening, I was hanging out with my other Scout honorees, Dave Knapp and Pascal Tessier. Looking a bit like three clowns at this event wearing Scout uniforms, we felt more comfortable sticking together. I did, however, spend some time mingling and talking to strangers and making new acquaintances. Michael went in a different direction for a while. Later, he told me he'd been engaged in conversation much of the evening with Edie Windsor trading stories about our lawsuits.

There were some great musical performers, most notably Debra Harry, who put on an impressive and crowd-pleasing show in a tight venue. I could tell Michael was really enjoying the experience, as was I, but I was also fighting my illness and struggling at times to stand and engage with coherent speech. After the event I would see pictures of myself there, pale as a ghost. I thought, what is that corpse doing there? When the gala came to an end, most were heading to an official after-party at a nearby club, but I told Michael I'd reached my limit. So we walked back to the hotel in the dark and bitter cold and called it a night. It was a remarkable evening, but it was a little incomprehensible we'd been included in that scene.

The next day, after we got back to Kentucky, I went immediately to the urgent care center, where I was diagnosed with double bronchitis. I started medical treatment, grateful it wasn't any worse than that.

In early December, I sent Edie Windsor an email congratulating her on being named as a finalist for the *Time* magazine Person of the Year award. She replied on December 4, 2013: "Dear Greg and Michael: I wish you two the very best outcome and—even more—the very best and happiest life together. Love, Edie Windsor."

In another exchange a few days later, she invited us to come visit her in New York. I very much regret we never got a chance to act upon that. As we were fighting our lawsuit for marriage equality in Kentucky, I can't tell you how much encouragement we received in our exchanges with Edie. She'd laid the federal groundwork for what we were trying to get done in Kentucky. What an inspiration!

Kentucky had another significant marriage equality event in 2013 unrelated to our lawsuit. A friend and co-worker of mine, Reverend Maurice Blanchard, and his partner, Dominique Harlon James, attempted to get a marriage license in Jefferson County Court. When they refused to leave after being denied, they were arrested. It was a brave act of civil disobedience that brought local and national attention to the issue of same-sex marriage.

On November 25, Maurice and Dominique were slated to be in court to face a judge over charges related to their arrest. Michael and I decided to attend in support of our friends. It was consoling to see how the court treated them so sympathetically. The judge ruled they had in fact broken the law and were guilty but fined them just one cent as a penalty. It was a great moral victory for the marriage equality movement in Kentucky and left everyone hopeful about our prospects in U.S. District Court.

Just a few days later, Maurice asked me if he could get our attorney's email address. He said he had a few questions for her regarding his next steps and hoped she could point them in the right direction. The request seemed a bit odd, and I wasn't sure where he was heading.

Dan Canon informed the Kentucky plaintiffs on December 17 that he had filed our brief and was waiting on the opposition filing. That started a very quiet waiting period ending up lasting a couple of months.

We waited through the holidays and early winter, during which I managed to work in a trip to Houston to participate in the annual Creating Change Conference. Creating Change, put on each year by the National LGBTQ Task Force, brings together LGBTQ leaders from across the country to hold seminars, share best practices, and foster collaboration. That year there was a panel of Scouts for Equality leaders who presented on our successful advocacy efforts to persuade the BSA to change its youth membership policy. The presenting team was one of the very best at that conference. It included my friends Charles Spain, Pascal Tessier, and Eric Andresen. Conference attendees received with enthusiasm their story of successful advocacy efforts with the BSA. Fresh off that big win, the BSA had just started allowing gay members the month before, so the Scouts for Equality team generated considerable interest at the conference.

18

JUDGE HEYBURN'S DECISION

For weeks our attorneys were engaged with filing legal briefs and participated in conference calls with Judge Heyburn to finalize the presentation of the case. On the morning of February 12, 2014, Michael sent out an urgent email that went to all four of the Kentucky plaintiff couples to let everyone know he'd received a call from Shannon. The judge's decision in *Bourke v. Beshear* was going to be released at noon that day. Shannon was in court, so she asked Michael to get the word out to the plaintiffs and ask any who could to meet at her office for a 3 p.m. press conference.

There was never a hearing that involved the plaintiffs. The attorneys did most of the work, and based on my notes and a re-review of my email history, it was largely done by document submission and phone, but not in person. There were some hearings with the judge but those only involved the attorneys. Of the four state cases that became *Obergefell v. Hodges*, only the Michigan case had a court trial that involved the plaintiffs.

There followed a flurry of emails among the plaintiffs with questions. Can we talk about the ruling before then? Will it be televised at noon? What can we say and not say? Finally, Dawn replied to the group by email at 11:22 a.m.: "It should be on Wave 3. We are under Order not to release the ruling to the public until noon. However . . . . . in my opinion, you are all Plaintiffs and not the public so . . . . WE WON!!!!!! WE FREAKING WON!!!!!!"

Somehow the press knew it already, too (how do they do that?), because I got my first media request from the local NPR channel two minutes later. The Clay Daniel Walton & Adams offices were only a few blocks away from my work. I got an urgent text to join a press conference there because the media wanted to speak to the plaintiffs. I walked in only knowing that the judge had ruled in our favor. I had not read Judge Heyburn's decision, so it was a little difficult to discuss it, but the attorneys there helped guide us through the opinion. When that was over, I decided there was no way I could go back to work under those circumstances, so I headed directly over to the Fauver Law Office.

The media hadn't yet arrived, so we started reconfiguring the furniture again in the conference room to accommodate the anticipated crowd, as we'd done for the initial filing. Gradually the other plaintiffs arrived, and we had our first opportunity to celebrate our winning decision together. The national media was already calling in, and all the plaintiffs participated in a tag team press conference. It was such a jubilant day. The plaintiffs were united with our attorneys in our joy and sense of relief and accomplishment.

In his opinion, Judge Heyburn discussed relevant legal issues related to the likes of Social Security and workers' compensation benefits that were affected by Kentucky's refusal to recognize same-sex marriages. He also wrote about income taxes and inheritance rights. Judge Heyburn expressed that the plaintiffs were not in any way in opposition to traditional marriage. Instead they should simply be permitted to benefit from its rights and privileges.

The most memorable quote from his opinion ridiculed the state's argument that it would be too expensive for to the state to allow same-sex couples to get married: "These arguments are not those of serious people." They are, he continued, "at best illogical and even bewildering." He concluded that he was presented "no other conceivable legitimate reason" for Kentucky's marriage ban on same-sex marriage and that it was in his legal opinion illegitimate.[3] After the decision had been rendered, local politicians started responding. Most were against the decision. Senator McConnell (R-KY) predictably condemned it. Even our

---

3. *Bourke v. Beshear*, No. 14-5291 (6th Cir. 2014), February 12, 2014, https:// law.justia.com/cases/federal/appellate-courts/ca6/14-5291/14-5291 -2014-11-06.html.

progressive Kentucky Democratic politicians were wary about supporting it for fear it might not stick, so they didn't want to go on record in favor of it.

The ball was now squarely in the court of Governor Beshear and Attorney General Conway. We would have to wait and see if they were going to let the ruling stand and become law, or if they planned to appeal to the U.S. Court of Appeals. In some other states, Democrats had let favorable District Court marriage equality rulings stand without challenging them. Collectively we thought that, with other state precedents, along with the fact that Beshear and Conway were Democrats, they might let the ruling become law without further challenge.

While we were waiting for that decision with our co-plaintiffs, in mid-February Michael and I again participated in a local annual event called Catholics for Fairness. We'd been going to this event for several years, but that year we were feeling particularly enlivened by the spirit. The event consists of a rally, a pilgrimage march for several blocks through downtown to our Cathedral of the Assumption, and then attendance as a group at Sunday evening Mass. Its goals were to influence the archbishop of Louisville to support LGBTQ equality under the law, and to raise awareness of and promote solidarity with LGBTQ Catholics. In previous years the event had been held outdoors, typically in bitter cold February weather, but the 2014 version was moved indoors to the Volunteers of America headquarters on Fourth Street.

The crowd's mood was ecstatic. Everyone was joyous over the recent ruling on recognition of same-sex marriage. Michael and I rejoiced in the sense of freedom the participants expressed over having won that first battle in U.S. District Court. We rallied, we marched to the cathedral, and we all prayed in thanksgiving that God seemed to finally be leading his marginalized and persecuted LGBTQ people out of the desert.

A few days later, on February 26, the U.S. District Court in Louisville issued its official ruling that a stay (sought at the last minute by the defendants) would not be in effect to delay its positive ruling in our favor.

IT IS HEREBY ORDERED that to the extent K.R.S. 402.055, .020, .040, and .045 and Section 233A of the Kentucky Constitution act to deny validly married same-sex couples equal recognition and benefits under Kentucky and federal law, those laws violate the

Equal Protection Clause of the Fourteenth Amendment of the United States Constitution, and they are void and unenforceable.

This is a final and appealable order.

John G. Heyburn II, Judge
United States District Court[4]

Of course, this was the desired ruling that a stay would not be ordered, but of course Judge Heyburn pointed out the ruling was appealable. Funny thing about appeals: they don't happen automatically. People have to ask for them. We held our breath to see who if anyone in Frankfort was going to raise their hand and request the appeal. Since the primary defendants in our case were Democrats, we plaintiffs and our attorneys were hopeful the changing climate toward accepting marriage equality in our state and throughout the country would sway them to consider accepting the District Court ruling and not appeal.

Our attorney, Dawn Elliott, praised the ruling to the media. She stated, "It's a great day to be from the Commonwealth of Kentucky. I hope that the attorney general and governor that I voted for don't jump on the appeal bandwagon."[5]

The next day the case took a slightly different shift. Judge Heyburn had made a statement in his ruling that his decision dealt only with the issue of same-sex marriage recognition from other legal jurisdictions. It did not apply to the issue of marriage licensure for same-sex couples who would like to get legally married in Kentucky. Judge Heyburn suggested he would have been willing to offer a similar opinion on licensure, but he had not been asked to do so with our case.

Very quickly our attorneys mobilized and recruited two longtime partnered but unmarried couples to file an *intervention* in *Bourke v. Beshear*. Couples Tim Love and Larry Ysunza, and the previously mentioned Maurice Blanchard and Dominique James, asked to be allowed to

---

4. Judge Heyburn, "Bourke V. Beshear—Final Order And New Filing Schedule," February 27, 2014, http://www.joedunmanlaw.com/blog/2014/2/27/bourke-v-beshear-final-order-and-new-filing-schedule.

5. Brett Barroquere, "Same-Sex Marriage Now Legally Recognized in Ky," *ABC News*, February 27, 2014, but see https://www.seattletimes.com/nation-world/same-sex-marriage-now-legally-recognized-in-ky/. See also https://mail.religioustolerance.org/hommarky4.htm.

intervene in the suit because licensure would use essentially the same arguments and could be addressed expeditiously. Judge Heyburn accepted this intervention, and the additional case named *Love v. Beshear* became a *legal bifurcation* of *Bourke v. Beshear*.

As that new drama played out, the Kentucky plaintiffs waited patiently for signs from the governor and AG as to which way they might be leaning. On the morning of Tuesday, March 4, one of our co-plaintiffs, Kim Franklin, sent out an email to the plaintiff group notifying us that AG Conway was going to make a formal statement that morning. It would be covered by local media and streamed live over the Internet. Because of the late notice, we couldn't get our group physically together, so we all just stayed in place and watched for the announcement. At work in the Humana Tower, I blocked off my calendar for the time the announcement was expected to be made. I closed my office door, said a little prayer, and fired up the Internet livestream, not knowing what a truly remarkable piece of political and social theater I was about to see.

AG Conway started his press conference by saying that he and Governor Beshear were the technical defendants and it was his duty to provide the commonwealth with a defense. He stated his office had respectfully fulfilled its duty to voters by effectively providing that defense. However, he pointed out it was also his duty to uphold both the Constitution of Kentucky and the Constitution of the United States. The temporary stay his office received four days earlier had given him time to confer with his client (Governor Beshear) and consult with state leaders about his decision. Having evaluated Judge Heyburn's opinion, Conway decided he would not appeal or pursue any additional stays, thus allowing the ruling to become law. He stated plainly that "from a Constitutional perspective, Judge Heyburn got it right."[6]

Sitting alone in my office, I covered my mouth in disbelief. My head sunk as I felt a great burden being lifted from my shoulders. I believed this was finally over, and Michael and I could just go back to living our normal lives again.

Looking away and then back to the camera, Conway continued that in light of other federal rulings across the country, it was not likely any of those appeals would be successful. "We cannot waste the resources of

---

6. Kentucky Attorney General Jack Conway, Press Conference, March 4, 2014, https://www.youtube.com/watch?v=xUqqUCPAOYg&t=28s.

the office of the Attorney General pursing a case that we are unlikely to win," said Conway. He recognized and spoke about those who feel as attorney general he had a mandatory responsibility to pursue an appeal, but he concluded that if he did so he "would be defending discrimination, and that I will not do."

The U.S. Constitution is designed to protect the rights of all Americans, both the majority and the minority. AG Conway said that he prayed over his decision. In making this disclosure his voice started to quiver. He talked about those he consulted in making his decision, including his "remarkable wife," Elizabeth. After that he paused at considerable length, head down, sniffling ever so slightly, then continued: "In the end, this issue is really larger than any single person, it is about placing people over politics. For those who disagree, I can only say that I am doing what I think is right. In the final analysis I had to make a decision I could be proud of, for me now, and for my daughters' judgment in the future." AG Conway then abruptly walked away from the podium without taking any questions.

As I sat alone in my downtown office with the door closed, my mouth agape, I started thinking about Jack Conway's very young daughters and how proud they will be of him in the future for taking that difficult and historic stand on the right side of history. What a remarkable man Jack Conway proved to be, weighing his daughters' future judgment in his decision. It is a remarkable elected official who will draw the line at discrimination and choose to put people over politics. He had to know the decision would be a great burden on his political career in Kentucky, but he chose to do the right thing.

Emails of congratulations and celebrating victory started to fly among our plaintiffs and attorneys. Shannon Fauver invited everyone over to her law offices at 2:30 p.m. to celebrate. Then something truly dreadful and unexpected happened. At 10:57 a.m., the Kentucky plaintiff group received a one-line email from our attorney, Joe Dunman: "Apparently Governor Beshear is hiring outside counsel to appeal the ruling."

What? We were dumbfounded. The AG has the final word on state legal matters. He had just quite publicly declared he would not appeal. We argued whether it was even possible for Governor Beshear to do that. Our attorneys were even more disappointed than the plaintiffs. They probably realized more quickly what had happened, and that our work was not over, it was just beginning.

Within minutes I received a couple of phone calls from local reporters asking if I could meet them and discuss this development in an interview. Within the hour Michael and I were expected to be at the Metro United Way Tocqueville Society luncheon at the Seelbach Hotel in downtown Louisville. I told a few of them if they wanted to get a statement, they could catch Michael and me there about thirty minutes before the luncheon. When we arrived, there were several local TV reporters waiting for us. They had set up for a TV interview in the lobby of the Seelbach. Other Tocqueville members were entering the hotel and were gaping at the spectacle because they did not even realize we were involved in the marriage equality lawsuit. When we spoke with the reporters, we expressed our satisfaction and gratitude with the AG's decision not to pursue an appeal but also our great disappointment and dismay over Governor Beshear's decision to take it upon himself to hire legal counsel for the appeal against the opinion of the AG.

The discussion continued in emails over the rest of the day. Not only were the plaintiffs and attorneys complaining about the Democratic governor's decision, but Beshear was also taking lots of heat from the mostly liberal local media for personally taking on the mantle of discrimination. Many people were angry with him and expressed this in many ways, but, of course, Kentucky being Kentucky, he also received a lot of conservative support. The following day, March 5, 2014, Michael sent a note to the Kentucky plaintiffs:

> I had told Greg recently that I was surprised about the number of people who I would have thought would be cheering us on were silent. I had taken their silence as lack of support or disagreement. Their silence apparently was not from lack of agreement and support!
>
> The governor's action has brought them out of the woodwork! Quite a few co-workers and friends who were silent have told me that they have contacted the governor. I have had lots of calls and emails from GE retirees and former employees to my work phone telling me they are proud and to keep up the good work!

To which I answered with my own email response: "Opposite response here at Humana today. The hate mongers came out on our internal Facebook (Humana's social media employee sharing site) called Buzz. Someone started a thread and several chimed in about Conway not doing his job, how Beshear was a hero, about how the people spoke in 2004 (when the people of Kentucky overwhelmingly—75%—voted to pass a state constitutional amendment banning same-sex marriage and defining marriage as being between one man and one woman), and some other disturbing comments. Our site administrator had to shut down the thread and delete it. I did not need that today."

Undoubtedly Kentucky was divided over the issue and this ruling. It was clear that because of Governor Beshear's politically defensive move, this case was going to live on and go to the United States Court of Appeals for the Sixth Circuit. We licked our wounds and waited for the next round to begin.

19

PREPARING FOR ROUND TWO

At the same time these lawsuit events were unfolding, I and others within Scouts for Equality continued to lobby organizations to stop funding the BSA. In early March 2013, Disney gave into pressure and decided to cut funding to BSA. The list of socially conscious corporate citizens withdrawing BSA funding grew to include Lockheed Martin, Caterpillar, Major League Soccer, Merck, Intel, UPS, Alcoa, AT&T, and others. These entities publicly ended their partnerships with the BSA over its continued resistance to full LGBTQ inclusion.

While lobbying for more change in the BSA policy, I also continued to participate in my parish troop activities and support the day-to-day operations of our scouting unit. There was great optimism that the BSA would very quickly follow its youth membership policy change and institute an adult membership change, but everyone acknowledged it was important to keep the pressure on the organization.

Suddenly it was late March, and Michael and I realized spring break was coming up fast for our high school children. That year we had a sophomore and a freshman in high school. Although we had been taking them to Destin, Florida, for spring break for many years, we knew they were getting too old for us to do that safely with the growing party scene for high schoolers there. We had observed the older high school students at Destin over spring break for many years and knew we did not want our teenagers to have exposure to that particular environment. As an appealing alternative we planned a spring break trip to New York City. The kids were okay with that because they had not been there before and it gave them the opportunity to experience the Big Apple. With all the commotion and stress related to the lawsuit, it was a great time for our family to get away, relax, and spend some time together.

Later, back in Kentucky, the calm thankfully continued for several weeks. The end of the school year was approaching fast, and I was busy planning the troop's annual Boy Scout drive to collect donations door-to-door for our local Crusade for Children charity. Each year our troop collected for three consecutive nights with our local fire department, and I had coordinated that effort for several years. At the same time, I was also planning once again to take the Scouts to summer camp the first week in July, a task that always consumed many weeks of planning and preparation.

Because June is Pride Month, I also felt inspired to recruit a Boy Scout honor guard to march in the Louisville Pride Parade. With some coaxing, a friend of mine from the U of L LGBT Alumni Council, Eagle Scout Scott Thompson, agreed to join Isaiah and me in the honor guard. A Scouts for Equality friend from Columbus, Ohio, Brian Peffley, also made the trip down to join us in uniform. Some other local scouts also participated, including a few active youth Scouts, but they were reluctant to break scouting rules and wear their uniform for this event. The parade crowd warmly received our group because of all the Scout-related media attention over the year and the BSA's past LGBTQ discrimination. The weekend after Louisville Pride, I also managed another trip back to New York City to participate in the first-ever Scouts for Equality honor guard at the New York Pride March.

Just before I was getting ready to head off to Scout camp, on July 1, 2014, our attorney Laura Landenwich informed the Kentucky plaintiffs that Judge Heyburn had released his favorable decision in the *Love v. Beshear* case, which had been filed as an intervention to *Bourke v. Beshear*. The original Kentucky marriage equality case, *Bourke v. Beshear*, sought recognition in Kentucky of legal marriages from other jurisdictions, while the *Love v. Beshear* case sought direct licensure in Kentucky for same-sex marriage. Laura stated: "As predicted, he found that Kentucky cannot deny marriage licenses to same-sex couples. More interestingly, he found that homosexuals are a quasi-suspect class entitled to height-ened scrutiny." This was encouraging and something our attorneys had hoped would develop because it suggested the government should add homosexuals to group categories such as gender and national origin when considering issues of equal protection under the law.

In his opinion, Judge Heyburn wrote:

> Sometimes, by upholding equal rights for a few, courts necessarily must require others to forebear some prior conduct or restrain some personal instinct. Here, that would not seem to be the case. Assuring equal protection for same-sex couples does not diminish the freedom of others to any degree. Thus, same-sex couples' right to marry seems to be a uniquely "free" constitutional right. Hopefully, even those opposed to or uncertain about same-sex marriage will see it that way in the future.
>
> The Court's holding today is consistent with *Bourke*, although it requires different relief. The ability to marry in one's state is arguably much more meaningful, to those on both sides of the debate, than the recognition of a marriage performed in another jurisdiction. But it is for that very reason that the Court is all the more confident in its ruling today.[7]

The Kentucky plaintiffs and attorneys were naturally quite thrilled with this decision, but we were also waiting to hear from the U.S. Sixth Circuit Court of Appeals about when arguments on *Bourke v. Beshear* would be heard. Shannon Fauver informed the plaintiffs after a few more weeks of waiting that the attorneys believed oral arguments would take place on August 6 in Cincinnati. She recommended that we all attend. The Sixth Circuit had decided that the Kentucky case would be argued jointly with similar marriage equality appeal cases from the three other states in the Sixth Circuit: Michigan, Tennessee, and Ohio.

Each state's case was to be given one hour and in succession. One attorney from each side of the argument would be given half an hour to make their case and answer questions from the judges. Four hours, eight attorneys, three judges, and thirty-seven plaintiffs (14 same-sex couples,

---

7. *Love v. Beshear* ruling: Judge Heyburn, July 1, 2014, http://ftm-assets .s3.amazonaws.com/ftm/archive/files/images/LovevBeshearRuling.pdf, 18–19; see also http://www.freedomtomarry.org/blog/entry/federal-judge-in -kentucky-strikes-down-marriage-ban.

2 singles whose spouses were deceased, and 7 children). Each of the four states still had separate cases at this point, with unique story lines and issues and different collections of plaintiffs. It was going to be a marathon and not a sprint for sure.

The hearing was set for August 6, 2014, at 1 p.m., but we were instructed to arrive and check in at the courthouse by 11 a.m. Given these circumstances, nearly all of the Kentucky plaintiffs decided to travel up the day before and spend the night in Cincinnati so we could be fresh and ready to go. Our children were out of school for the summer. Naturally Michael and I thought this would provide them an incredible life experience, so we decided to take them along. There was a little concern about how the teenagers would handle four to five hours stuck in a courtroom without digital screens, food, or the ability to even use the restroom, but we did not want them to miss this once-in-a-lifetime experience.

The interest in the Sixth Circuit hearing started building nationally. In late July the Freedom to Marry organization, founded by Evan Wolfson, contacted Michael and me because it was preparing profiles of the various marriage equality plaintiffs and they wanted to include us. After our profile was published, we received a surprising amount of moral support, but the one that was most endearing was this July 25, 2014, email:

Dear Greg (and family):
[W]hat a beautiful story and how heart warming. Congratulations and love and best wishes for your success in the next step.
I'm rooting for you.
Edie Windsor

20

SIXTH CIRCUIT COURT OF APPEALS

As the August 6 day of reckoning approached, the attorneys and plaintiffs were really feeling the stress. There was considerable discussion about which attorney was going to argue for Kentucky's plaintiffs in Cincinnati. The initial set of plaintiffs were fiercely loyal to and supportive of Shannon Fauver and Dawn Elliott, who originated the case in the first place. However, the attorneys from Clay Daniel Walton & Adams had deeper civil rights experience and wanted an opportunity to argue this high-profile case in the Sixth Circuit Court of Appeals. There was a bit of a power struggle, but the plaintiffs felt a bit distanced from much of the maneuvering. In the end, it was decided that Laura Landenwich would argue the case. Michael and I were initially disappointed it wasn't Dawn or Shannon, but we also wanted the best person for the job. It became apparent among the Kentucky attorney group that Laura was that person.

In advance of the court date, the Why Marriage Matters Ohio group contacted us. It was organizing a pro–marriage equality rally the night before the hearing at Lytle Park in downtown Cincinnati. They wanted plaintiff representatives from each of the four states to speak at the rally. I was tapped to represent the Kentucky plaintiffs and speak on their behalf. Although I had spent some time talking to the media, I still was very uncomfortable speaking to larger crowds, so the prospect was unnerving.

Then there was another wrinkle. Some of my friends from Scouts for Equality in Cincinnati were organizing a Scout honor guard as part of the program for the rally on August 5. The previous year I had marched in Scout uniform in the Scout honor guard at the Cincinnati Pride Parade, so Scouts for Equality wanted me, as a plaintiff, to participate in the flag team for the rally. It is always a great honor to participate in uniform in a flag ceremony, but it was especially meaningful for me to do so that night.

After presenting the colors and posting the flags, I joined the other plaintiffs and attorneys backstage to wait for the program to commence. It was a bit awkward being in my Scout uniform while everyone else was in regular street clothes, but it appropriately reflected the dual causes for which I was actively engaged at that time: marriage equality and equality and inclusion in scouting. When it was my turn to speak to the crowd, I explained how Michael and I had been together thirty-two years and worked and raised our family in Kentucky nearly all those years. We had earned the right, I argued, for our union to be recognized legally, just like any other married couple. The plaintiffs on stage with me were all Kentuckians, and we were calling on our state to end its discrimination against LGBTQ people.

It was a great relief to get that task behind me and then enjoy the rest of the rally as the other state plaintiffs and attorneys took turns revving up the crowd. It was an uplifting night, a satisfying one, and one that gave us great hope and optimism for the court arguments the next day.

The morning of oral arguments, Michael and I arose early and had breakfast at our hotel with our kids, then we went about the routine task of getting cleaned up and dressed. We were keenly aware that people were always scrutinizing us as gay parents as to how we were doing raising our children. That day we took special care to ensure our children were thoroughly cleaned, dressed for church, and ready to face the world. When our family arrived at the courthouse, there was already a large group of supporters rallying outside and a substantial crew of media. A few of the television stations from Louisville had sent reporters over to Cincinnati, and we all enjoyed seeing and speaking with those familiar and friendly faces that day.

At the appropriate time, our attorneys herded us away from the rally outside and moved us toward the check-in station inside the courtroom. We left behind a large group that was still rallying. They were to hold a march through downtown Cincinnati while the hearings were going on inside.

As we approached the security station, just in front of us were our three attorneys from Clay Daniel Walton & Adams. We barely spoke, for two reasons. They were clearly just as stressed out as we were, but also we were still a little unhappy that Laura Landenwich had been chosen to argue the case and not one of our initial attorneys, Dawn Elliott or Shannon Fauver. It felt a little childish not trying to connect, but they seemed to be just as cool to us that day. Later I would reflect on that nonencounter and regret I didn't try harder to be friendly and supportive, especially since Laura did such an extraordinary job that day representing our case.

After making it through the check-in station, we meandered through the massive federal structure that is the Potter Stewart United States Courthouse, which fully consumes a large city block in the heart of downtown Cincinnati. After entering the courtroom, we were reminded again about the rules. Once the oral arguments started, no one would be permitted to leave for any reason except during official breaks. We would have to be completely silent. All personal phones and devices would have to be turned off. Basically, we were told to sit silently for four hours and don't say a word or do anything but concentrate on the proceedings. Michael and I were fine with that, but we just didn't know if our teenagers would be up to that challenge. Thank goodness the proceedings that day were so entertaining that our children were fully captivated by the arguments.

Court day also presented the opportunity for many of the plaintiffs from Michigan, Tennessee, Ohio, and Kentucky to meet in person for the first time. Settling into our seats, we introduced ourselves and briefly shared stories. There were young couples and old couples and a surprising number of children in attendance. By my recollection the courtroom seated only about 250 people. Every seat was taken in that small but dignified space. There was excitement in the air and much nervousness.

The Circuit judges assigned to hear and decide the cases were Martha Craig Daughtrey, Jeffrey Sutton, and Deborah Cook. Our attorneys did not brief us in advance on who exactly would be hearing case arguments, so we were unprepared for what we were walking into. The Sixth Circuit Court of Appeals had the reputation of being perhaps the most conservative in the country. Later we found out that Judges Sutton and Cook had both been nominated by President George W. Bush and both had long records of very conservative decisions. Neither was seen as friendly to the LGBTQ community. Judge Daughtrey, who was nominated to the Circuit Court by President Bill Clinton (and who was also born and raised in Kentucky) proved to be the only voice of reason on the bench that day.

Our Kentucky case featured attorney Laura Landenwich. She argued against Governor Beshear's counsel Leigh Gross Latherow, who was from a prominent law firm in Ashland, Kentucky. The Michigan case featured Aaron Lindstrom from the Office of the Michigan Attorney General against Carole M. Stanyar, who was representing the Michigan plaintiff couple, April DeBoer and Jane Rowse. William L. Harbison, of Sherrard & Roe in Nashville, represented the Tennessee plaintiffs. That state's interest was spoken for by Joseph F. Whalen from the Office of the Tennessee Attorney General. Finally, Alphonse (Al) Gerhardstein argued for the Ohio plaintiffs against Eric E. Murphy from the Office of the Ohio Attorney General.

Other than Laura, Michael and I did not know any of these other people or their reputations before getting started that day, but we certainly grew to know and respect all of them by the end of that long day.

I found a lot of the arguments silly. They either discussed concepts of equality and equal treatment at a level way over our heads or nitpicked over the meaning of specific words. Given that each of the eight attorneys had very limited time for presentation and questions, things moved pretty quickly. The speakers and the arguments changed rapidly, so there was no time to get bored, nod off or even daydream if you wanted to keep up.

Judge Cook was surprisingly very passive during the entire day. I only remember her asking one question, and it was so neutral that it gave no clue as to what she might be thinking or how she might be leaning. The other two judges? Well, they had plenty of questions and plenty to say.

Judge Sutton repeatedly said that it might be better for the culture and the institution of marriage if the LGBTQ community worked toward changing "hearts and minds" to secure marriage equality rather than have it forced on the public through a court decision. It was clear from his comments and questions he did not feel this was a matter the courts should decide. He implied the people had already decided through their state constitutional bans and in state legislatures. It should be the people who decide to institute marriage equality and not the courts, he argued. By the end of the day, we knew exactly where he stood. He would be leading the charge against the plaintiffs.

Joe Dunman, one of our Kentucky attorneys, later wrote in his blog:

> The oral arguments in the Sixth Circuit were extremely civil, without the sharp contrasts in opinions among the judges evident in the Fourth and Tenth Circuits. Judge Cook was mostly silent. Judge Daughtrey was highly critical of the states defending the bans. But Judge Sutton, the lead judge on the panel and considered by most as being (or at least having been) a top conservative prospect for a [U.S.] Supreme Court nomination, balanced his questions between both sides. He suggested to the same-sex marriage plaintiffs that the political process could be a better route for equality rather than the court system, but acknowledged the long history of discrimination they suffered and was unsympathetic toward state arguments about tradition and legal confusion.[8]

The breath of fresh air we plaintiffs all fell in love with that day was Judge Martha Daughtrey. Several of her comments and questions had the courtroom laughing vigorously. Her humor and wit frequently helped to diffuse what was a very tense environment.

Two exchanges stood out. First, after the argument and discussion about taking the "change hearts and minds" approach, she abruptly asked the Ohio state attorney if he knew how long women had struggled for the right to vote before it was won with the Nineteenth Amendment. The attorney was surprised by the question and could not answer, so Judge Daughtrey told him it took nearly a century of efforts at the local, state, and national level for women to fully gain the right to vote. Boom! It was a remarkable piece of courtroom drama, much better than anything I ever saw on *Perry Mason* when I was growing up.

The other notable exchange was between Judge Daughtrey and Governor Beshear's attorney, Leigh Latherow. Judge Daughtrey was frankly confused by the Kentucky argument that it must prohibit same-sex

---

8. Joe Dunman, "The Sixth Circuit Waiting Game," October 17, 2014, http://www.joedunmanlaw.com/blog/2014/10/17/the-sixth-circuit-waiting-game.

couples from marrying to ensure procreation and the survival of the human race. That was in Kentucky's interest? Just the long pause and look on her face of *are you kidding me?* was priceless, not to mention the tone of her voice, which seemed to say, *You can't expect me to take this seriously, can you?* Her levity and pointed questions certainly won over many hearts and minds that day.

The arguments drew to a close and, with everyone emotionally exhausted and in need of a potty break, we were all dismissed. The Al Gerhardstein law office of the Ohio plaintiffs was across the street from the courthouse. They had graciously invited the plaintiffs and attorneys from all the states to come over for a reception. Michael and I were really tired and had to work the next day back in Louisville, but our children were hungry, so we decided it would be a good idea to come on over just to get a bite to eat before hitting the road. There was a great sense of relief and accomplishment among the attorneys and plaintiffs. Mostly we were just grateful to have the hearing behind us. After a beer and a few bites of food, the Bourke De Leon family was thrilled to be headed back home and put that stressful but necessary event in our rearview mirror.

After we returned to Louisville, we realized it was time to get back into the school year grind with the kids. There was so much to do: books and supplies to buy, clothes and uniforms for the kids' Catholic high schools to update, and generally getting back to normal life. It was a good feeling to put behind us the stress that had built to a maddening crescendo those days before the hearing. The boring, simple life of work and school brought our family comfort and healing through the late summer and into fall.

No one knew precisely when the decision from the Sixth Circuit would come. We tried not to think about it or talk about it much. With same-sex marriage decisions all over the news, we couldn't help following some of the other Circuit Courts across the country, wondering if or when the first "split" would happen that might launch an appeal to the U.S. Supreme Court. All of the District and Circuit decisions rolling in were in favor of marriage equality. The conjecture was that Supreme Court would not take up an appeal from a Circuit unless there was a split or reversal from the District to Circuit level.

With marriage equality on the back burner, I returned to lobbying Metro United Way (MUW) more vigorously to stop funding the local Lincoln Heritage Council (LHC) of the BSA because of its antigay discriminatory membership policy. MUW was saying the right things, indicating it would pull funding for the LHC. Chris Hartman of the Fairness Campaign and I had several meetings with Joe Tolan, its executive director. He assured us they were moving to defund LHC.

As Scout councils across the country were losing their United Way funding over this issue, the BSA came up with a most deceitful workaround. It had founded a wholly owned separate 501(c)3 nonprofit, and operations were set up in all major cities with a Scout council. The Learning for Life organization was organized as a "career skills building program" that used BSA office space and was staffed with BSA shared leadership. Since Learning for Life was a quasi-independent organization, it was able to sign the MUW nondiscrimination agreement to satisfy MUW and receive funding.

We had no doubt the $170,000 awarded to Learning for Life in its very first year of operation in Louisville would actually be diverted to fund LHC activities. Chris Hartman and I challenged both organizations for their participation in this highly questionable maneuver. We wrote an op-ed exposing this deceit that was published in the *Courier-Journal*.[9] We also organized a protest at the MUW Annual Campaign kickoff event at Churchill Downs the second week of September. It drew considerable media attention. It was a real embarrassment for MUW's leadership to have local corporate leaders attending its celebratory campaign kickoff event while walking through a boisterous antigay discrimination protest. As a MUW Tocqueville Society member, I was very uncomfortable to have to do this to my friends there, but I felt they really needed to be held accountable for their actions.

As time wore on, we realized we'd soon have to deal with the inevitable decision from the Sixth Circuit. We had to be prepared to react, win or lose. On September 12, 2014, Chris Hartman and I received an email from Michael Aldridge, executive director of the ACLU of Kentucky. He dove into the delicate subject of how and where to gather after the decision was made public. Other local and regional organizations were asking what it was going to do. ACLU of Kentucky wrote:

---

9. Greg Bourke and Chris Hartman, "Boy Scouts, United Way Playing Trick on Supporters," *Courier-Journal*, July 19, 2014, https://www.courier -journal.com/story/opinion/contributors/2014/07/19/boy-scouts-united-way -playing-trick-supporters/12848135/.

As you know, when we passed on being involved at the trial level of these cases many people were unhappy with us, and some remain that way. While we've come on board at the circuit court level, we've never wanted to try and take the spotlight away from the hard work done by so many others or to give that appearance. Because the ACLU plays a role on LGBTQ equality nationally and both the ACLU and the Fairness Campaign do the statewide work here in KY, we often receive media calls for comment, but we've been careful not to try to take credit where it is not due.

So while we would support and attend any big gathering to celebrate a victory in the 6th, it seems inappropriate for us to coordinate such an event. If we did, we would invariably be seen as trying to take credit.

A very sore spot with the Kentucky plaintiffs and attorneys was the lack of support from the ACLU, both national and especially ACLU Kentucky when we filed our case and as it worked its way through the courts. Even today, most people don't realize the lack of support at the beginning. When Michael and I filed our case with our two initial attorneys Shannon and Dawn, for the longest time it felt like it was just the four of us against the world. We were shunned, criticized, and ridiculed for our efforts. It was discouraging, to say the least.

Even as more plaintiffs and attorneys signed on to the case, we still lacked any substantial support from local, regional, and national gay rights organizations. So, when Michael Aldridge wrote this note and acknowledged the history and did so in very conciliatory manner, we saw an opportunity to let the past go and start working together for a successful future. I was given the task of taking that message of reconciliation and selling it to the other Kentucky plaintiffs. A couple of plaintiffs had a very negative response, but for the most part the plaintiffs agreed that it would be advantageous to put forth a united front, no matter what the outcome from the Sixth Circuit.

Perhaps the best response that day came back from fellow plaintiff, Tim Love, who wrote: "I personally spoke to the attorney in charge nationally for marriage equality at ACLU at the Cincinnati rally. He apologized and said it was his fault as he was trying to efficiently use resources where they felt they had [the] best chance to win. It sucks but we can't blame them for skipping over Kentucky. Maybe they will think twice before leaving us behind in the future. Valuable lesson for us to remember. Don't wait for any national organization to ride in and save us."

As we waited for the results from the Sixth Circuit, the marriage equality movement continued to move successfully through other federal courts. A watershed day occurred on October 6, 2014, when the U.S. Supreme Court let lower court rulings stand and refused to hear appeals from five more states that had had their marriage bans swept away: Indiana, Oklahoma, Utah, Virginia, and Wisconsin. The decision not to hear the appeals also meant that six other states in the same category—Colorado, Kansas, North Carolina, South Carolina, West Virginia, and Wyoming—would also soon have their marriage bans removed.[10]

Those changes would increase the number of states recognizing same-sex marriage from nineteen to thirty. Circuit Court of Appeals rulings were still in the works for the Sixth, Ninth, and Fifth Circuits, and the Supreme Court still did not have the "split decision" that it was looking for to take up an Appeals Court case on a writ of certiorari. The way the Circuits were falling, many were speculating that every Circuit would rule in favor of marriage equality and that SCOTUS would not have to be the final decider of the issue. But those three outstanding Circuits were all considered pretty conservative, so no one was ready to claim victory until we got the final word.

Within a couple of days after neighboring Indiana gained marriage equality, a surprising email arrived in my box on October 9, 2014, from the Gay and Lesbian Alumni of Notre Dame/Saint Mary's College announcing "Breaking News: Notre Dame and Saint Mary's to Provide Same-Sex Partner Benefits":

> GALA-ND/SMC commends the University of Notre Dame and Saint Mary's College for announcing that they will immediately extend partner benefits to legally married same-sex couples. The announcements come after the U.S. Supreme Court declined to hear appeals from decisions striking down bans on same-sex marriage in several states, including Indiana.

---

10. By Adam Liptak, "Supreme Court Delivers Tacit Win to Gay Marriage," *New York Times*, October 6, 2014, https://www.nytimes.com/2014/10/07/us/denying-review-justices-clear-way-for-gay-marriage-in-5-states.html.

At Notre Dame, all eligible faculty and staff were notified of the major change in policies on Wednesday night via email. "This means that the law in Indiana now recognizes same-sex marriages and the University will extend benefits to all legally married spouses, including same-sex spouses," the email to employees stated.

This was an unexpected and remarkable development, since Notre Dame and Saint Mary's had vigorously fought to deny same-sex partner benefits. As Catholic institutions, they felt it dogmatically necessary to hold the line on same-sex marriage. But after the state of Indiana was required to recognize marriage equality, the two institutions seemed to fear an onslaught of lawsuits if they did not also comply. The fact that Notre Dame was not challenging this decision was noteworthy, but even more notable was that its faculty and staff in same-sex marriages would finally receive employment benefits for partners, especially healthcare.

Back at my workplace, Humana was also engaging in my fight with the MUW and the BSA. Even back in 2014, Humana was a staunch supporter of LGBTQ rights. Since I was one of the founding members of our Humana Pride Network Resource Group, I had some influence over matters. Humana had a long history of supporting MUW with an annual campaign. It was consistently one of the largest corporate campaigns in the city. Since I'd gone to great lengths to shine the light on the deceptive Learning for Life funding by MUW, and because several other associates also raised concerns over this deception, the Humana Foundation and its leadership informed MUW it would launch a thorough review of the situation. It was a veiled threat, but it was fabulous to see that my employer was dedicated to both organizational integrity and support for its LGBTQ associates.

21

REVERSAL

On November 6, 2014, at precisely 4:29 p.m., Michael forwarded an unexpected email to me at work that he'd received a minute earlier. It was from a marriage equality plaintiff friend in Texas. "6th Circuit Reverses," it said. There was no other text, but an official Sixth Circuit document filed moments earlier was attached. Michael had passed it on to the Kentucky attorneys and plaintiff group. Our collective hearts sank. It wasn't over, again.

The attorneys took over. Laura Landenwich calmed us and said she was reading it thoroughly. Joe Dunman told us it was public and word was getting out. Shannon Fauver replied she was reading it and would have feedback soon. Dan Canon instructed everyone to remain quiet until a good legal position for a response could be developed so we could present a united front and common message.

But it was hard to remain calm. We had lost. Victory had been snatched away from the righteous. We had let down the rest of the LGBTQ community.

Fear surfaced about what it would mean for the other states that already had marriage equality by court decision. Would those be rescinded? Would they be reversed? There was never a sense of certainty regarding our victory, but the plaintiffs had not thought that much about defeat and what it might mean not just for us but for many others. It was a dreadful feeling, and we all went into a collective funk. Seconds later I received a form email from Michael Premo of the Campaign for Why Marriage Matters Ohio:

This isn't the news I was hoping to share, Greg:

Moments ago, the 6th Circuit Court of Appeals upheld Ohio's refusal to recognize legal marriages of same-sex couples who married in other states. And to make matters worse, the 6th Circuit also did not strike down marriage bans in Michigan, Kentucky and Tennessee.

This ruling flies in the face of 38 pro-marriage rulings—including rulings from three other Circuit Courts of Appeals—since just last year's *Windsor* case.

My heart sank again. How could we let everyone down like that? This couldn't really be happening. Then my cell phone rang and it was Chris Hartman. He wanted to let me know that Fairness Campaign was going to have a rally at noon the next day at City Hall in support of marriage equality and wanted me to get the word out to the Kentucky plaintiffs and attorneys. That task at least distracted me from the doubt and self-blame that had started to consume me.

Then just a little after 5 p.m., attorney Dan Canon got back to us all with his legal take:

The bottom line is:
1. We are still reading and analyzing the opinion, so we cannot make comment on any specifics at this time (clients, you can just refer those questions to the lawyers).
2. We basically have 3 options: ask the same panel to review it; ask ALL the judges on the 6th circuit to review it, or ask the Supreme Court to review it.
3. We are weighing our options and coordinating with other states, so we do not know what action we will take as yet.
4. We are disappointed, and we think the ruling is wrong, but we do not intend to let it go unchallenged.

Laura Landenwich subsequently offered hope to the plaintiffs: "We will continue the fight. The 6th circuit's view that fundamental rights should be subject to majority vote is dead wrong. Also, to quote Judge Daughtrey in her dissent: 'the majority sets up a false premise—that the question before us is 'who should decide?'[11] . . . In point of fact, the real issue before us concerns what is at stake in these six cases for the individual plaintiffs and their children, and what should be done about it."

Attorney Dawn Elliott offered, "We can strategize but I feel like asking the 6th Cir for anything else will not be a productive use of time and won't get a different result. Shannon talked to a clerk at the Supreme Court. . . . it seems they await our request and would like it swiftly." Dan Canon closed the circle for us. The attorneys, he advised us, all seemed to be thinking about the same SCOTUS option, but he needed to confer with the other three state teams to see what their intentions were regarding follow-up options with the Sixth Circuit.

The legal opinion to fight the decision was presented to the plaintiffs, but there was still uncertainty about which option offered the best path forward. After I read Dan's statement about possibly asking the Supreme Court to review it, it was truly the first time I recall letting myself think it might actually become an option. In the back of my mind over those preceding months I knew the possibility was out there, but I honestly believed we would win the Sixth Circuit. Just like at District Court, we would win the same way we'd done in every other Circuit that had ruled to that point. They'd all come down in favor of marriage equality. I wanted this all to be over, so I hadn't seriously entertained the thought that the fight would continue past the Sixth Circuit and on to the U.S. Supreme Court. At that point, the stars had unexpectedly and strangely aligned. An appeal to the Supreme Court appeared to be inevitable.

Later that evening Adam Polaski of the national Freedom to Marry organization offered his condolences to the Kentucky plaintiffs:

We were all sorry to read about the 6th Circuit Court of Appeals' decision from this afternoon, and as you and your team work to figure out next steps in the fight to win marriage for same-sex couples in Kentucky, I wanted to reach out and let you know that Free-

---

11. *DeBoer v. Snyder*, Sixth Circuit Court opinion: DAUGHTREY, SUTTON, and COOK, Circuit Judges, "Opinion: Nos. 14-1341/ 3057/ 3464/ 5291/ 5297/ 5818 DeBoer v. Snyder," UNITED STATES COURT OF APPEALS FOR THE SIXTH CIRCUIT, November 6, 2014, https://www.opn.ca6.uscourts.gov /opinions.pdf/14a0275p-06.pdf, quote at 43.

dom to Marry would be more than happy to support your team and pitch in where we can. We are more committed than ever to winning marriage for same-sex couples nationwide, and we are thankful for plaintiffs and legal teams like yours who are doing such important work.

Just after that, Freedom to Marry founder Evan Wolfson followed up "to underscore our willingness to work with and help you, as we've done with the other legal teams in the states that had reached the Supreme Court in the last round."

When it finally appeared the Sixth Circuit cases were headed to the Supreme Court after all, some of the national LGBTQ rights organizations began to pay more attention to these cases from the flyover states. It was welcome support indeed since many of us were feeling a bit in over our head at that point.

On Saturday, November 8, 2014, Shannon Fauver emailed the Kentucky plaintiffs to let us know that all the attorneys were working through that weekend to ready the petition for the Supreme Court filing. She said the other three states were going to do the same. That news set off speculation among the Kentucky plaintiffs and attorneys about whether the Supreme Court would accept just one of the state cases, or two, or consolidate all four of them into one. Kentucky was the only state that had two cases addressing both the marriage recognition and marriage licensure question, so naturally our attorneys thought if just one state was selected, it would be Kentucky so there would be a more comprehensive decision.

As the attorneys went about their legal business, I finally had a chance to read through the lengthy Sixth Circuit decision. I'm not an attorney, so a lot of the legal arguments went over my head. Judge Sutton was consistent with many of the same themes he presented personally in court.

In his written opinion, Sutton stated, "This is a case about change— and how best to handle it under the United States Constitution. From the vantage point of 2014, it would now seem, the question is not whether American law will allow gay couples to marry; it is when and how that will happen."[12] Sutton cited the rapid changes that had brought

12. *DeBoer v. Snyder*, 7.

nineteen states to decide in favor of marriage equality. In his opinion, he suggested that marriage equality was a freight train. It couldn't be stopped. He just didn't think he should be the one to make that decision.

After reading his opinion, I began to respect the fact that Sutton esteemed the institution of marriage so much that if it was going to be radically and irrevocably updated, it needed to be done by a higher power: the U.S. Supreme Court.

Judge Daughtrey in her dissenting opinion was quite critical of the decision:

> But as an appellate court decision, it wholly fails to grapple with the relevant constitutional question in this appeal: whether a state's constitutional prohibition of same-sex marriage violates equal protection under the Fourteenth Amendment. Instead, the majority sets up a false premise—that the question before us is "who should decide?"—and leads us through a largely irrelevant discourse on democracy and federalism. In point of fact, the real issue before us concerns what is at stake in these six cases for the individual plaintiffs and their children, and what should be done about it. Because I reject the majority's resolution of these questions based on its invocation of vox populi and its reverence for "proceeding with caution" (otherwise known as the "wait and see" approach), I dissent.[13]

A couple of weeks passed. The plaintiffs were getting restless, and we all started asking our attorneys about when our petition for appeal to the Supreme Court was going to be filed. On November 16, Shannon Fauver notified us that the petition was at the printer and would be delivered to the Supreme Court the next day. It was such a relief. The attorneys had warned us that if they missed the filing deadline, they'd have to wait for the Supreme Court's next session to take up our petition for consideration. Along with Kentucky, the other three Sixth Circuit states all managed to meet the deadline and similarly filed their petitions. The hardest part was over. It was now a waiting game to see if SCOTUS would accept the case. The attorneys told us it could be as early as January before we'd hear anything.

---

13. *DeBoer v. Snyder*, 43.

To celebrate the successful filing, Shannon suggested we get the whole Kentucky plaintiff and attorney group together for drinks and dinner the second week of December. We settled on meeting at the Silver Dollar, a local pub with a casual atmosphere located pretty much right across the street from Dawn and Shannon's law office.

The day we were supposed to meet, the plaintiffs received an email update from attorney Joe Dunman. He let us know that "our case is currently set for the conference of January 9, 2015. During that conference, the Justices will discuss our case and could decide to grant certiorari then. They could also decide to pass the case to a later conference if they decide they want to wait for some reason. They could also decide to deny cert. We have still not been granted certiorari, so there is still a possibility that our case could be rejected. In other words, at this moment in time, we are not yet up for review."

Getting that news made our group gathering that much more exhilarating because we had a date to focus on and a better understanding of what the possible outcomes might be. Processing those options and hoping we would get the green light, the plaintiffs were hopeful we could get past this task as soon as possible.

That night, as all the Kentucky plaintiffs and attorneys gathered at the Silver Dollar, we talked strategy and possible outcomes. Nothing too heavy came out of it, and there were no major decisions made. But the evening gave us the chance to get together in person and bond instead of interacting disjointedly through email chains. It was a warm, cordial gathering of friends and collaborators. We definitely needed to strengthen our bond and steel our nerves for whatever might be coming our way after the holidays.

The next week I enjoyed an inspiring exchange of emails with Edie Windsor after I informed her about the scheduled review date at SCOTUS. In her December 17, 2014, email she told me, "Best wishes is all I can say, and I mean it from my heart. I'll hold my breath throughout January. Edie"

It is impossible to express just how much it meant to receive Edie's support during this period and to know she was rooting for us. She'd been through all this herself not long before when she took her successful fight to the Supreme Court to declare the Defense of Marriage Act (DOMA) unconstitutional in *United States v. Windsor*. Edie had become an instant icon in the LGBTQ community after her stunning victory. I think she realized our pending case was going to finish the job and deliver marriage equality for the whole country. We were all holding our breath in advance of that decision.

The holidays came on fast. The Supreme Court became the furthest thing from our minds. Michael and I were busy with decorating, shopping, and parties. There were also lots of Boy Scout activities, which always ramp up when everyone's out of school with time on their hands. We had our family traditions for the holidays. For example, we always went to Christmas Eve Mass at 4:30 p.m. I regularly took the opportunity to serve as Communion minister captain at that festive service. The holidays that year were a blessing for our family and allowed time spent together away from work and school, with hardly a thought or word about any pending lawsuit. It was just a traditional family celebration of the birth of our savior Jesus Christ with the rest of our faith community and extended family.

After the holidays, in early January 2015 the national ACLU contacted our attorneys. It wanted to start working with Kentucky's plaintiffs and attorneys before SCOTUS made any decision about accepting our case. Many of the plaintiffs participated in an ACLU conference call as a group. Michael and I had a follow-up call with ACLU media strategist Crystal Cooper. She coached us on some ACLU talking points and other tips specific to our case that we could use when talking to the media. After going it alone at District and Circuit Courts, we found great comfort in having a professional PR person prepare us for what might eventually become a very stressful and challenging situation. It was also reassuring that the heavyweight national organizations were finally starting to get behind the case as we got closer to a possible courtroom showdown.

After a long wait, on Friday, January 16, 2015, the Supreme Court issued its notice that it was granting the petitions for writs of certiorari for the four state marriage equality cases:

> The cases are consolidated and the petitions for writs of certiorari are granted limited to the following questions: 1) *Does the Fourteenth Amendment require a state to license a marriage between two people of the same sex?* 2) *Does the Fourteenth Amendment require a state to recognize a marriage between two people of the same sex when their marriage was lawfully licensed and performed out-of-state?* A total of ninety

minutes is allotted for oral argument on Question 1. A total of one hour is allotted for oral argument on Question 2. The parties are limited to filing briefs on the merits and presenting oral argument on the questions presented in their respective petitions.[14]

At that point the ball was back in the attorneys' court. Briefs had to be filed by February 27, 2015. A representative from the Humana HR Department contacted me immediately to ask if I knew of any companies filing *amicus* briefs in support of marriage equality. Humana wanted to join as a sponsor or signee. That outreach really warmed my heart. My employer wanted to step up and take a strong position to support both marriage equality in general and me personally.

As February drew to a close, the Kentucky plaintiffs and attorneys were evaluating ideas, such as taking a chartered bus to Washington, DC, for oral arguments (we didn't); having a fundraiser to cover some of the plaintiff/attorney travel costs (we did fundraise but ended up donating the proceeds to Fairness Campaign); and where we would all be staying in DC. The attorneys also had a growing concern that there may not be enough tickets for all six Kentucky plaintiff families and all five or more of our Kentucky attorneys to be seated during the argument. That launched a lot of discussion about who should go or not go and who should be seated in the SCOTUS courtroom for arguments.

Initially, we couldn't believe the Supreme Court couldn't seat all our entourage. Later we learned the courtroom was actually a somewhat modest space and there were rules about ticket distribution. In addition, general demand for this highly anticipated session would be through the roof. Several of our plaintiff families raised concerns about not wanting to finance an expensive trip to DC, especially if a seat in the courtroom could not be guaranteed. We were all in a tizzy over who would get seats and who would not. That uncertainty persisted for several weeks before the picture finally cleared up.

Around that time, Crystal Cooper at the national ACLU started circling back around. She was getting more and more engaged with the Kentucky plaintiffs. She wanted to dispatch an ACLU photographer

---

14. Supreme Court of the United States, "(ORDER LIST: 574 U.S.) CERTIORARI GRANTED," January 16, 2015, 1–2 (emphasis added), https://www.supremecourt.gov/orders/courtorders/011615zr_f2q3.pdf.

from New York, Molly Kaplan, to come to Kentucky and take some photos of some of the Kentucky plaintiff families before the national media got interested in the oral arguments. Michael and I had welcomed quite a few other reporters into our home over the years, so we agreed. Our working relationship with the ACLU continued to grow deeper.

In another unexpected development, Stanford University's Supreme Court Litigation Clinic contacted our attorneys. It wanted to help the Kentucky legal team prepare petitioner briefs. It also offered to bring our entire group of Kentucky attorneys and plaintiffs to San Francisco to participate in two days of strategy sessions, planning, and panels related to the case. It was a generous proposal to assist us, and we all decided to participate. Jeffrey Fisher at the Stanford Law School coordinated our visit. Our team felt it was a great advantage to work with such an esteemed attorney. Fisher had an historic record of success leading winning marriage equality decisions in other states.

Our children were in school at that time, and Michael and I didn't want them to miss a couple of days of instruction, so we asked Michael's sister Debra to fly in once again to make sure our teenagers stayed on task. Thank goodness she was able to come. The trip to San Francisco turned out to be very fruitful for our legal team in its efforts.

Before we could get on the plane, in early March the Kentucky plaintiffs and attorneys received an email from Amanda Snipes, a campaign manager for Freedom to Marry. That organization was making the rounds throughout the South to raise awareness about the case and wanted to hold two town halls in Kentucky. One would be in Lexington on March 17 and one in Louisville on March 18. Freedom to Marry invited our Kentucky plaintiffs and attorneys to participate on a panel for both events. Evan Wolfson, who's considered the father of the marriage equality movement, was going to be speaking on the history and evolution of the movement at both events.

For many years, and especially during the early to mid-stages of *Bourke v. Beshear*, it had seemed like the rest of the marriage equality movement had ignored our efforts in Kentucky. All that changed after we were included in the SCOTUS case. Some of the Kentucky plaintiffs were a little put off that we'd been given such short notice about the Freedom to Marry events. On the other hand, we realized they could provide the public and needed forum where we could make our case and tell our stories in our home state. We were, after all, still in the business of changing hearts and minds.

Media interest was also starting to escalate, not just with the local newspapers and television but also national media. Many of the Kentucky plaintiffs and attorneys were slated for interviews. One that really worked out beneficially for Michael and me was a request from Amanda Terkel, politics managing editor at *Huffington Post*. Amanda was coming to Louisville in mid-March and wanted to meet with several of the attorneys and plaintiffs. Michael and I were glad to accommodate her, but the only time slot we had available with our busy schedules was on a Friday evening after work. Our only condition: Michael and I had already signed up to volunteer at a Lenten Fish Fry at Lourdes that evening. No problem. Amanda and her videographer seized the opportunity and met us at the Fish Fry. Amanda had the chance not only to speak with Michael and me at length but also interview several fellow parishioners. She even spoke with our pastor. They all had glowing things to say about us and our family.

Our pastor, perhaps fearing retaliation from the archbishop, who was opposed to same-sex marriages, was reluctant to speak on camera, but he did have one remarkable line. When asked about Michael and me in relation to Church policy toward gay people, he simply responded, "You see how they fit in." Imagine that. At a Catholic parish, all of these people were defending us and our family and supporting our efforts to bring marriage equality to Kentucky and the rest of the country. Amanda decided to promote that angle with her story, and it resonated well with her readers.[15]

Oral arguments were set for April 28, 2015, so the Kentucky team all independently made travel arrangements to get to Washington, DC, early. Adam Polaski of Freedom to Marry told us the group was planning a grand reception. The National Marriage Plaintiffs Gathering, for all marriage equality plaintiffs, past or present, from any state, would be held the evening before. Michael and I planned to attend with our children, as did the rest of the Kentucky team.

As the date of oral arguments approached, national media attention increased dramatically along with local interest. Nearly all of it was supportive. Rarely were there hard challenges from reporters about an alleged

---

15. Amanda Terkel and Christine Conneta, "They're Just Good People. And That's Kind of What It's All About, Isn't It?," *Huffington Post*, April 20, 2015, https://www.huffpost.com/entry/greg-bourke-michael-deleon_n_7024888.

gay agenda, religious freedoms, or the death of traditional marriage. But we did get our share of hate mail and an occasional threat. Much of the hostility was communicated via comments on media posts and in articles that we read. People will say such vicious and threatening things when they can do so anonymously and hide behind an online persona. We also had mail sent directly to our home anonymously and unmarked. Sometimes it was a religious brochure from someone who wanted to "share God's good news" with us, but occasionally the messages were more threatening and insulting.

The plaintiffs also felt plenty of love in those days from people who supported our efforts, but we were also the target of a lot of recrimination. I can't tell you how many nights I went to bed in fear, staring at the window and worrying if this would be the night a brick or fire bomb would come smashing through the window. By then I'd been openly gay for nearly forty years, and I'd spent most of my life looking over my shoulder in parking lots, living in fear of being targeted. The court case had drawn so much more unwanted attention to our family. My fears only increased by the day. I could not wait for this whole thing to be over so we could get out of the limelight and return to our calm, boring, and inconspicuous middle-class suburban lives.

Honestly, I have been one of the lucky ones. Or maybe it's because I partnered off in early life and that kept me away from potentially dangerous situations.

Coming out in the 1970s and going to the only two seedy gay bars in downtown Louisville, there was frequent violence against the patrons. People got beaten up, tires were slashed. Antagonizers from their cars would scream and taunt me as I went into the gay bars, and once someone threw a beer bottle at me, but I never got physically hurt. I never was the direct victim, but I was still touched from the persistent assaults on the gay community.

In the 1980s it was more of the same, whenever I or we went into any gay setting, we had to be ultracautious. People used to get targeted coming in and out of the bars, which were our only semisafe space for community. In addition, Kentucky sodomy laws were still active until 1992. Police often entrapped people or simply enforced the laws.

Then after becoming public advocates for gay rights, we would get hate mail, nasty emails, and so on. Whenever there was an article in the paper or a social media post about us, you would not believe the hateful and frightening things people would say. I'm feeling a little PTSD just writing this.

There was another incident a couple of years ago when our pastor called me over before Mass to let me know the parish center had received an anonymous phone call about us. The caller said that Muslims had it right about throwing gay people off of buildings to their death. Father Scott called the police to report it, but the caller was never identified. He wanted me to know and asked us to be careful. Thankfully, nothing ever came of that either.

I truly don't want people to think I've been a victim in my life. I was lucky. But many LGBTQ people really have been victims of violent and sometimes deadly attacks. But understand that whether one directly experiences that violence or not, many if not most LGBTQ people live with that relentless fear—especially people of my generation. In my case I had been out so long, it had probably been accumulating much longer than for most.

In the last days before leaving town, the ACLU contacted us about a press conference that was supposed to take place in DC on April 23, just a few days before oral arguments. It wanted the two of us to participate as representatives of Kentucky's plaintiffs. We'd be joining some of the Ohio plaintiffs at ACLU's offices in DC. We looked at our work schedules and our teenagers' commitments and decided there was no way we could both go, so we decided I should go while Michael took care of matters at home.

When I arrived at ACLU's offices in DC on April 23, I visited at length with Ohio's plaintiffs: Jim Obergefell; and Joe Vitale and his husband, Rob Talmas. Joe and Rob had brought their toddler son with them. Little Cooper was adorable and quite active. When the press conference started, we all took turns briefly telling our stories and why we had gotten engaged in the legal battle for marriage equality. Jim talked about his quest to have his husband's death certificate reflect that he died a married man. Joe and Rob discussed how it was important for them because the state of Ohio would not show both parents on their son's birth certificate. Their legal marriage was not recognized in Ohio.

My story was similar to Joe and Rob's but was unique because of our family situation. I described the anguish I felt being a parent and raising two kids for sixteen years while living in fear they'd be taken away from me if something happened to Michael. Remember, Michael was the only legal parent. That was always our story, our motivation for the case. We wanted to protect our children and our family by having our marriage recognized. Winning marriage equality would give our family the same protections that other families already had under the law.

Another topic of discussion was our lifelong commitment to the Catholic Church. Michael and I had raised our children in our faith and even sent them to Catholic schools. That revelation seemed to pique reporters' interest. That day I spent a considerable amount of time explaining why we felt that way.

After the press conference, I had a long conversation with Debbie Cenziper from the *Washington Post*. She was working with Jim Obergefell to write a book about the case.[16] Debbie asked if she could come visit us in Kentucky in a couple of weeks after the arguments so she could include more of our story in the book.

I also spent a long time conversing with Steve Smith, communications officer from the ACLU. Steve is also Catholic. He wanted to talk about how we reconciled it all, how we made it work being openly gay with our parish. People do seem to wonder about that. I frequently reflect on that also. Michael and I have spent more time than you can imagine defending our faith to people on all sides of the issue.

After the press conference was over, fellow plaintiff Jim Obergefell and I decided to share a ride to the airport. Jim's a remarkably kind and modest person. He was a bit apologetic over all the attention he was getting as the named plaintiff in the case, *Obergefell v. Hodges*. He was keenly aware we had a large plaintiff group of thirty-seven from four states, so he found it a bit awkward to often be the center of so much attention. I told him that from my perspective I was glad it was him and not me. I would not have had the time and focus to devote to the undertaking that he had. At times I felt I was barely holding things together through the whole ordeal. Home, work, church, and the media spotlight were all just too much. I can't imagine how much more of a burden it would have been if I'd been the named plaintiff in the case. Would I have wanted to be the focus of so much more scrutiny than the rest of us? Jim and I shared a hug and parted ways at the airport, knowing we'd both be back in DC in just a few days to start the final mad dash to the oral arguments.

---

16. Debbie Cenziper and Jim Obergefell, *Love Wins: The Lovers and Lawyers Who Fought the Landmark Case for Marriage Equality* (New York: William Morrow, 2016).

22

ROAD TRIP TO DC

No sooner did I get back to Kentucky than it was time to start packing up our fourteen-year-old Honda Odyssey minivan for the long drive to Washington, DC. Over the years we'd used that van for maybe eight spring break trips to Destin, Florida, countless camping trips with the Boy Scouts, a half dozen family trips to South Bend for Notre Dame football games, our marriage trip to Canada, and so much more. That trusty van had been our companion and transport to many Bourke De Leon family events and experiences, but it had never been on such a momentous trip to hear oral arguments at the Supreme Court. As we drove, we joked how, when we crossed the state line from Kentucky to West Virginia, all of a sudden we were recognized as married. We also talked about how nice it would be when we no longer had to worry about such things.

Rolling into DC on Sunday, April 26, 2015, we checked into our rooms at the Hilton Garden Inn. We selected those accommodations because we knew our friends and co-plaintiffs Randy Johnson and Paul Campion and their children would be there and we could all hang out together. It was also within easy walking distance to the Supreme Court.

After dropping our bags, we quickly made our way down to the Supreme Court Building just to see who was there and what types of protests or rallies might be going on. On social media we'd seen many of our friends check in from the Supreme Court Plaza. It was a bit of a carnival atmosphere. There did seem to be plenty of enthusiasm in the air when we arrived. We had a chance to visit with some of our friends and talk to many of the people who'd camped out in line for days in hopes of getting a seat for oral arguments.

Of course, there were protesters. Some had been setting up camp each day for weeks. We did our best not to engage with them, but they had bullhorns and were incredibly annoying and even provocative at times. Isaiah, our seventeen-year-old, was not having any of their antagonizing rhetoric. At one point he borrowed a large rainbow flag and defiantly walked past the protesters to help tamp down their message.

There were also several hundred people camping out in line in front of and around the side of the Supreme Court Building hoping to get inside on hearing day. Some were paid line-standers holding spots for people or organizations that wanted to secure a seat. Others were just highly motivated individuals who wanted to watch history being made as the Court took up this argument. We spent a couple of hours listening and talking with people in line who were swept up with the buildup to the big event in two days.

After our visit to the Supreme Court Plaza, we walked back to the hotel to prepare for a behind-the-scenes visit Sunday evening to the West Wing of the White House. Jeremy León, who worked in the White House Office of Management and Budget, and his husband, Bryan León, had arranged to give us and a few of the other plaintiffs a personal tour. Bryan and Jeremy were the first same-sex couple to be legally married in DC. They graciously contacted us in advance to set up the insider tour. Also on the tour were Jim Obergefell and some of his relatives, Joe Vitale and Rob Talmas and their son, and one other remarkable person we had not yet met, Anthony Sullivan.

The tour was impressive, but the company was even better. Afterwards we all went for dessert and talked for hours about our different experiences. Michael and I were blessed that night to be seated with Anthony Sullivan and to hear in his own words his incredible life story. Tony and his longtime partner, Richard, were among the very first same-sex couples in the country to attempt legal marriage. That was in Boulder, Colorado, in 1975. Tony, an Australian citizen then, used that marriage to apply for U.S. citizenship, but the federal government refused to recognize it. It was an inspiring story indeed, and after finishing dessert and conversation, Michael and our restless teenagers and I went back to our hotel for the evening and to prepare for another full schedule the next day.

We spent several hours the following day, Monday, back at the Supreme Court Plaza, talking to supporters, other plaintiffs, many attorneys, and some media. There was great anticipation and confidence in the air, but the protesters were also ever-present, reminding us there was still tremendous opposition to marriage equality. Not wanting to miss out on the opportunity, we also walked up and down the National Mall to visit the Washington Monument and the Lincoln Memorial. A few years before, our family had spent a spring break vacation in DC and there were a few of the iconic sites we wanted to revisit. It also gave our family a little peace and a break from all the hubbub at the Plaza.

There was a photo shoot later that evening on the steps of the Supreme Court Building for all of the thirty-seven plaintiffs and dozens of attorneys that made up the *Obergefell v. Hodges* case. To prepare for that, we walked back to our hotel to get dressed for the photo and the nationwide Plaintiff Reception that would follow. When the plaintiffs and attorneys all arrived back at the Plaza, a lot of cat-herding ensued. How do you get fifty people lined up for a photo that would include the Supreme Court Building? Eventually the photographer ended up with a few good pictures that captured the size and diversity of our group.

After wrapping up, we took a taxi to the spacious and well-appointed Holland & Knight legal offices in downtown DC. Security was tight. When we got off the elevator, the space was already packed and very loud. There was a lengthy queue for taking photos behind a banner celebrating the event. After that we spent the next couple of hours with our children circulating the space and meeting many of the marriage equality plaintiffs who had not been included under the Sixth Circuit Court of Appeals decision. We swapped stories with plaintiffs from Mississippi, Indiana, New York, Oklahoma, and many others in addition to spending time with our fellow Kentucky plaintiffs and attorneys. All told there were seventy-five plaintiff couples from across the country. Unfortunately we didn't have time to meet them all.

A brief program included speakers from the Obama administration and Evan Wolfson, whose Freedom to Marry organization was hosting the reception. The evening was a chance for many of the plaintiffs to meet personally for the first time. They'd all been working for so many years toward this moment. It allowed us to connect the dots, to see how plaintiffs were connected, and to learn how so many had worked so hard to build on previous struggles at different times and places. There was a feeling of unity in purpose with our shared goal of achieving marriage equality for the entire country. We all felt perched on the brink of achieving that goal.

23

MICHAEL'S BIRTHDAY, AND ORAL ARGUMENTS TOO

Anyone with teenagers knows it can be challenging to get them up for anything early morning. That was our task on April 28. Up early, shower, prep, get dressed appropriately for a morning appointment in the U.S. Supreme Court. The ACLU had created a war room for all attorneys and plaintiffs to use during the day at the Capitol Hill Hotel a few blocks from the Court building. Everyone was invited to gather there before heading over to court and to use it to collaborate during the day. Our family arrived as requested at 8 a.m. and settled into the space. The Reverend Maurice Blanchard, our Kentucky co-plaintiff and a Southern Baptist minister, led us in prayer before breakfast. It was sustenance we'd need as we sat through several hours of pre- and post-courtroom time.

The first question the Supreme Court was going to address that morning was licensure. *Could the states refuse to allow same-sex couples to marry?* After a brief break, the second session would take up the separate question on *recognition of legal marriages from other jurisdictions.* Two of our Kentucky plaintiff families were seeking licensure and another four Kentucky families were seeking recognition, so we were split into groups along those lines. Each plaintiff family would attend only the session relative to its specific circumstances. (The licensure question went first, then the recognition.) That was one concession we had to make so that everyone could attend the arguments.

Sadly, not all of our attorneys could secure seating that day, and it really bothered us. I was particularly upset that one of the attorneys we started our journey with, our dear friend Shannon Fauver, could not secure a seat. Shannon selflessly opted out, but thankfully Dawn Elliott did get in. It was comforting to see that friendly and familiar face in such a stressful environment.

Attorneys Joe Dunman and Dan Canon were our assigned handlers that morning. They coordinated getting our first-session Kentucky families collected, transported, and passed through Supreme Court security, and they generally served as needed guides during the events of the day. The first-session plaintiffs were escorted down the street and into the courtroom, and the second-session families remained at the Capitol Hill Hotel a while, talking and awaiting our turn to begin the walk over to court. The minutes passed like hours as we waited. When it was time, Joe Dunman gathered the rest of the second-session plaintiffs together and led us on the walk over to the court where we would hear oral arguments on this recognition. I had forgotten, or perhaps not considered, that there would be a rather large crowd rallying in the Plaza to show support.

As we approached the Plaza, Michael and I held hands for much of the walk. That was something we have rarely done in public over the years, being of our age and from our generation. As we entered the Plaza, we got swept up in the crowd a bit but knew we also needed to stay together. Since our group couldn't be seated until the Question 2 session, we were able to attend part of an enormous pro–marriage equality rally on the Plaza. Speaker after speaker gave rousing justification for the Court to rule in favor of marriage equality once and for all. It was a great pep talk for the plaintiffs before we entered.

Security was tight. After checking through entry, we were escorted to the Supreme Court's cafeteria to wait. Since seating was limited in the courtroom itself, many of the plaintiffs' children couldn't be seated. They, along with our two teenagers, would have to wait in the cafeteria with some of the attorneys to watch over them.

After a brief wait, we were moved to the next staging area, a hallway on the first floor with a large open space up to the second floor where the courtroom is. We had to stay in a restricted area, and our security detail kept herding us back onto the carpet area. As we waited and softly chatted, loud shouting from the courtroom on the second floor shattered our quiet. It went on for about a minute. Later we learned it was an anti–marriage equality protester who had to be forcibly removed from the building. Needless to say, the shouting and scuffle was just one more thing to unnerve us.

Our co-plaintiffs, Paul Campion and Randy Johnson, were our friends long before the lawsuit, so we waited with them for the first session to end. After a few minutes we were moved from our safe space on the carpet to a single-file line up a long narrow stairwell leading to the second floor. As we stood on the stairs, I remember talking to Paul about how nervous I was and how it felt like I was even trembling on the inside. Passing through another security line, we had to proceed to upstairs lockers and leave various personal items forbidden in the courtroom, such as cell phones. We were also told we could not display any pins on our lapels or jackets. I had to remove an ACLU pin and a Freedom to Marry pin and place those in my coat pocket.

Eventually all second-session plaintiffs were queued up again outside the courtroom's entry doors to wait for the order to enter. The first-session plaintiffs had already left. As we entered, the first thing I remember was the blast of warm air that hit me in the face. It was almost May in DC, so the temperature outside was already rising to summer levels. The courtroom had been packed—really packed—with hundreds of people for a couple of hours, so it was no wonder it felt so oppressive.

I had never studied photos of the Supreme Court and the courtroom before. Given the stature the institution holds in our government, it was a surprisingly small space. After walking through the doors, we proceeded down a narrow aisle toward a couple of rows of open seats. Every eye in the place was on us as we took our seats.

It was an overpowering feeling. The stares didn't necessarily imply judgment or support. It was just a moment when I realized how many people were keenly invested in that day's proceedings. Every minute detail, every word, every action was being carefully scrutinized. There was nowhere to run, nowhere to hide, so what else could we do? We took our seats.

Despite my anxiety over the proceedings, I never felt physically safer in my life. There was so much security but particularly in the courtroom itself. Ubiquitous agents in black suits stood alertly in all the aisles. Our attorneys had cautioned us at check-in that the Court would tolerate no speaking or any disruptions. The security team made sure all eyes and all attention were firmly placed on the panel of justices on the dais at the front of the room.

Because the space was so modest, we felt like we'd landed some really great concert tickets right up front. As we looked at the bench, we didn't even have to squint to see very clearly the faces of each one of those famous justices. It felt like we were sitting face-to-face. Even though we did not speak directly, it felt as if we were in direct conversation with the justices the entire time.

Justices John Roberts, Anthony Kennedy, Ruth Bader Ginsberg, Antonin Scalia, Elena Kagan, Sonia Sotomayor, Samuel Alito, Stephen Breyer, and Clarence Thomas were household names held in the highest esteem. There they were, sitting right in front of us as they prepared to hear arguments about marriage equality. It was hard to even process at that time. It felt a little bit like watching a movie of someone else's court drama. Facing the justices, I remembered its 5–4 votes in the Prop 8 and *Windsor* cases and consoled myself that the Court had not changed any justices since those decisions. This case was the next logical step. As I looked directly at those nine justices, I knew who had voted for and against those previous decisions. I paid very close attention to each of them and exactly what they were saying and asking, looking for clues about who might flip with this round of questioning.

Douglas Hallward-Driemeier, an attorney we'd seen in action at mock trial arguments in Louisville, argued Question 2 for the plaintiffs. He was a very formidable and most persuasive orator. Chief Justice Roberts did a brief open and introduced him. Doug began by arguing that the petitioner couples were already married and no state should be able to nullify what another jurisdiction had already sanctioned. Because of those marriages, Doug argued, we had built lives and families around the presumption we were in fact married with all that entails. He did not get very far into his argument when Justice Alito interrupted him with a question. Then Justice Scalia challenged whether this same argument would also apply if people were allowed to marry polygamously in one state or to a twelve-year-old in another. Would other states have to recognize those marriages?[17]

---

17. Supreme Court of the United States, "No. 14556 JAMES OBERGEFELL, ET AL., Petitioners v. RICHARD HODGES, DIRECTOR, OHIO DEPARTMENT OF HEALTH, ET AL." Alderson Reporting Company, April 28, 2015,

It was a frustrating line of questioning, but these types of arguments had been raised for years. They stirred fears of "slippery slopes." Where does it stop? Then there were questions about incest. It was exasperating to listen to the justices comparing what we knew as loving, committed long-term same-sex marriages to other highly questionable relationships that are widely recognized as harmful and illegal. After a lifetime of hearing those arguments, it was refreshing and reassuring to hear our attorney, a staunch straight ally for marriage equality, defending us against those charges. He understood why those questions were being asked, and he knew exactly how to respond.

After those exchanges, Doug spoke directly to the state of Kentucky's position. The state's argument, if the Court accepted it and the plaintiffs lost, implied we might walk away from our existing same-sex marriages and enter into opposite-sex marriages to procreate. Doug described that idea as not a rational justification. Kentucky's argument really was a head-scratcher. If the state recognized out-of-state same-sex marriages, would it lead to a decline in the number of children born into marriages in Kentucky? I wanted to raise my hand and say, look, we already have two adopted children and have no interest in procreating additional ones at the ripe old age of fifty-seven. But I restrained myself.

Chief Justice Roberts weighed in. He said that the states have had the right to regulate and protect marriage. In doing so, can they maintain some prohibitions against some forms of marriage? Justice Roberts and Hallward-Driemeier engaged in quite a back and forth for a while. At that point, I got the sinking feeling that Roberts was not going to flip from his dissent in *Windsor* in favor of marriage equality. He was the one fairly moderate justice who, I thought, might have a chance of moving his position during arguments, but it didn't look like he was going to be convinced.

Several of the justices, including Alito, Ginsberg, and Sotomayor, started a new line of questioning. What would be the next challenge for traditional marriage after same-sex marriage? After they repeatedly pressed him, Doug reluctantly settled on age restrictions. That put Doug in the position of having to defend age-related state marriage restrictions

https://www.supremecourt.gov/oral_arguments/argument_transcripts/2014/14 -556q1_l5gm.pdf; https://www.supremecourt.gov/oral_arguments/argument _transcripts/2014/14-556q2_8m58.pdf.

while carefully and meaningfully differentiating such relationships from same-sex ones. He did a remarkable job. I think he managed to persuade everyone with his explanation.

Doug had one remarkable argument. If opposite-sex couples beyond child-rearing years moved to another state, would they be entitled to have their marriages respected? That scenario was essentially no different from what we were seeking. He further argued that we plaintiffs took marriage very seriously or we would not have sought out that designation and secured it for our families.

Tying a nice bow on his splendid performance, Doug wrapped up, and Chief Justice Roberts turned the floor over to Joseph Whalen, who argued for the defendants.

Whalen barely got started when Justice Scalia interrupted him. He quoted Article IV of the Constitution, which requires states to give full faith and credit to the public acts, records, and judicial proceedings of the other states. Scalia pressed Whalen on why that should not apply in this case. It seemed to me that he was arguing precisely why states should have to recognize all marriages from other states. While Doug had been arguing, the mood in the courtroom had been serious. But when Whelan took over, there was initially a lot more levity and laughter as the justices seemed to be toying with Whalen and some of his arguments.

There was an extraordinary discussion about what if licensure were defeated but recognition was endorsed, or vice versa. What would that mean? A challenge came from the bench. Were arguments made in the licensure session being reargued or contradicted with the recognition statements? Again, I wanted to raise my hand and say, plaintiff here, can we please just focus on *this* question? Not that those weren't important queries to be considered, but it seemed the discussion was about everything but the practical importance of the case to specific plaintiffs who were simply asking their marriages be recognized.

Justice Ginsberg finally brought forth perhaps the most enlightening question of the day. She asked why a divorce decree in one state must be recognized in every other state, but the same does not and should not apply to an act of marriage? Whelan couldn't really come up with a convincing answer, but he did offer that parentage was based on the male–female relationship and had its foundation in biology. That argument had a lot of us perplexed. Several justices appropriately fired back with questions about adoption and infertility. All of the arguments against marriage equality that had been circulating for years were getting recycled in this one session. Thankfully, they did not appear to be compelling anyone to side strongly with the anti–marriage equality sentiment.

With some relief, the session wound down abruptly and quietly drew to a close. We were adjourned. It was such an incredible relief to have oral arguments behind us. There were really no great surprises, blunders, or revelations. We felt confident that it boded well for our case.

The courtroom dismissed into the outer chamber, and plaintiffs started to gather together. Our attorney handlers directed the plaintiffs to retrieve phones and other personal belongings from the lockers and meet just inside the front door so Kentucky's plaintiffs could exit together as a group. Someone had decided plaintiffs would go out the front door alphabetically by state groupings with Kentucky first and walk down the iconic Supreme Court steps to a podium to speak to the crowd and address the media. After Michael and I went to get our phones, Paul Campion and I were detained by one of our attorneys who was trying to herd people together. We waited there just long enough to miss the stepping off of the other Kentucky plaintiffs out the front door. When we realized what happened, Paul and I sprinted down the steps to catch up with our families and the other Kentuckians, but we felt cheated that we didn't get to walk out the door and down the steps together as planned.

After all the plaintiffs and attorneys had made it down the steps, we gathered by a podium and took turns having one representative from each state give remarks. Just that morning at our war room breakfast, I was informed I'd been designated as the speaker for the Kentucky plaintiffs. Of course, that was a surprise, but as with everything else related to this case, I simply resolved to do my best. As I'd sat in the courtroom just minutes earlier listening to arguments, my mind had been racing. *What the heck am I going to say out there? What the heck am I going to say?* I struggled to both pay attention to the arguments and put together talking points to remember when I got outside. I can't recall what I said on that podium about Kentucky, the state where I was born and have lived most of my life, the state I love and where I will be buried. Kentucky needed to treat our legal marriages with respect. All of the plaintiffs deserved that from the Commonwealth of Kentucky. It was time to make that the law.

The other state plaintiffs had their turns and provided rousing comments, as did the attorneys who spoke for the plaintiffs in court, Mary Bonauto and Doug Hallward-Driemeier. Afterwards we broke into smaller groups and took turns doing interviews with the national press covering the event. The crowd remained large and quite festive. We thoroughly enjoyed engaging with the marriage equality supporters well into the afternoon.

Around 2 p.m., the plaintiffs had to start making excuses. Many of us walked together to the subway station to catch transport to an ACLU reception at its DC offices. It was a fitting way to finish the day, a private gathering of plaintiffs and attorneys where all could decompress and compare notes about what had just happened. Most importantly it allowed us all to just relax. The arguments were over. We'd done everything we could have collectively done to advance the case and without major errors or missteps. Now all we had to do was wait calmly and patiently for the final decision.

After leaving the ACLU, the Kentucky plaintiffs' final stop was a visit to our U.S. representative John Yarmuth (D-KY) at his Capitol Hill office. When we arrived, John's staff treated us like royalty. They quickly ushered us into his office where we were offered drinks. Kentucky bourbon never tasted so good. It was certainly an appropriate beverage for the occasion. We raised our glasses and toasted a successful day.

There was a lengthy discussion about the case, about how conservative Kentucky was, and, of course, conjecture on when and how the Court would decide. Representative Yarmuth spoke to the plaintiffs about the new fronts for the progressive movement, which included medical marijuana and decriminalizing pot in Kentucky. He recognized how difficult it often is to lead Kentucky forward through progressive change. As a center-left Democrat myself, I was surprised to hear that issue springing forth from Yarmuth since it wasn't front and center in Kentucky in 2015. After a round of pictures with Yarmuth and thank-yous, the group dispersed. Though long and quite tiring, it had been a satisfying and eventful day.

Since our family was staying at the same hotel as the Johnson-Campion family, we decided to go out to dinner that night and celebrate. The valet had tucked our cars away, so we asked the concierge where we could dine within walking distance. There weren't a lot of options, but he offered the name of a family-style restaurant about a twenty-minute walk away. Although tired and hungry, we set off together, our family of four and the Johnson-Campion family of six, walking through downtown DC in a most delighted manner.

As we walked, our teenage children and the Johnson-Campion teenage children started a conversation about how they had feared getting mowed down outside the Court building by a gunman earlier that day. A bit stunned, we adults revealed we'd been concerned about the same thing. We had seen enough of the protesters at the Supreme Court Plaza to know there was a real possibility of violence. Someone might choose to act out against us. They perceived us as a real threat to conventional marriage. The fact we all had this thought, but none of us spoke about it during the day, showed how heavy this possibility weighed on our minds.

24

GOING HOME

The next morning, we gathered up the kids, checked out of the hotel, and started the long drive back to Kentucky. Everybody in the van mostly slept through the ten-hour drive while I drove and replayed over in my mind the developments from the previous day. At home, as we walked in the door, the phone started ringing. It was a local news reporter. We were thoroughly exhausted. Our first thought was, oh, great, here we go again. But actually the reporter was sharing news that Judge John Heyburn had passed away that day and he wanted to come to the house to interview us. Judge Heyburn had provided an eloquent defense for same-sex marriage in making his District Court ruling in *Bourke v. Beshear*. We owed him a great debt of gratitude, so we agreed.

The next day, the *Courier-Journal* newspaper asked us to write an op-ed tribute for Heyburn. Michael took the lead on that project and wrote a nice piece called "A Plaintiff's Appreciation of Judge Heyburn" that appeared April 30, 2015:

> Judge Heyburn ruled with justice and respect. His opinions were witty and intriguing, and included writing that the common person could understand: "In America, even sincere and long-held religious beliefs do not trump the constitutional rights of those who happen to have been out-voted." The rulings from Judge Heyburn were im-

mediately referenced by other judges as same-sex marriage cases swept the nation.[18]

We were deeply saddened by Judge Heyburn's passing but grateful for his service to justice. Our paths had crossed in such a meaningful way.

With the oral arguments of *Obergefell v. Hodges* over, it was time to get back to work. Our children had to return for the last few weeks of the school year. It had been an exhausting academic year with all the extracurricular activity related to the lawsuit. We kept them out of the media as much as possible, but the Supreme Court case for marriage equality was the talk of their respective Catholic high schools.

With our court date past us, I had the chance to slide back into scouting activities. During that time Robert Gates, president of BSA (and former head of the CIA and former U.S. secretary of defense), made a plea to the organization to end the ban on gay leaders because "we must deal with the world as it is, not as we might wish it to be."[19] Gates further stated he would not enforce the gay ban. This was a striking development. The media wasn't far behind. Jose Diaz-Balart of MSNBC called to see if I'd agree to an interview on his show, *The Rundown*. I put on my Scout uniform one more time to tell my story of discrimination and to advocate for the complete removal of the ban for lesbian and gay adult leaders.

Gates's decision inspired me to write a lengthy email to Barry Oxley, chief Scout executive at the LHC, to ask if he'd adopt a similar position and allow me to return to registered leadership. It went nowhere, but Brad Hankins of Scouts for Equality gave me some words of encouragement. In typical Scout fashion he reminded me that "without friction, no fire gets started."

Toward the end of May 2015, we started thinking more and more about the impending Supreme Court decision. Michael and I talked

---

18. Michael J. De Leon, "A Plaintiff's Appreciation of Judge Heyburn," *Courier-Journal*, April 30, 2015, https://www.courier-journal.com/story/opinion /contributors/2015/04/30/plaintiffs-appreciation-judge-heyburn/26625495/.

19. Erik Eckholm, "Boy Scouts' President Calls for End to Ban on Gay Leaders," *New York Times*, May 21, 2015, https://www.nytimes.com/2015/05/22/us/boy -scouts-president-calls-for-end-to-ban-on-gay-leaders.html.

about the possibilities. Speculation was that the decision would come down on or around the last day of the SCOTUS season at the end of June before the Court adjourned for summer break. Conferring with other Kentucky plaintiffs, we talked about who might be going to DC to be there in person for the decision. The Johnson-Campion family were the only Kentucky plaintiffs hoping to attend, but they were planning a long-scheduled vacation and couldn't guarantee they'd make it in time. The other Kentucky plaintiffs intended to stay at home and, they hoped, celebrate when the decision came down. It was left to our family to make plans for yet another trip to DC.

The main problem: we didn't know exactly when the Court would rule. If we waited too long, we might miss decision day. We coordinated our plans with James Esseks of the ACLU. That group wanted Kentucky representation since it had stepped up and supported us leading into oral arguments. On June 10, 2015, we also heard from the ACLU's Crystal Cooper: "While it's possible that SCOTUS rules on any Monday this month (with Thursdays, other days to be added soon), we're focusing our efforts on June 29th and 30th." It was the rampant rumor that the Court would rule the last Monday (June 30) of its session because it has done that with many other historic decisions.

James Esseks encouraged the plaintiffs to continue accommodating media requests and stick to ACLU talking points. One of those discussions ended up being a visit in our home from Colin McNulty from the BBC, who was doing interviews with as many of the *Obergefell* plaintiffs as possible. McNulty wanted the interview to focus on our lives as lifelong practicing Roman Catholics since he was covering religious objections to same-sex marriage. He seemed genuinely surprised and encouraged to hear our story and wanted to share the faith aspect of our journey with his listeners.

One other loose end that month was a trip to South Bend to participate on a panel at the annual Reunion Weekend at Notre Dame. For years I'd been a member of the Gay and Lesbian Alumni of Notre Dame/ Saint Mary's College, also known as GALA ND/SMC. GALA put on an academic panel at Reunion each summer to discuss current and historical aspects of LGBTQ student life at the conservative Catholic college.

In 2014, when I participated in a Reunion panel for the first time, I was struck by the frustration LGBTQ people and their allies in the audience were feeling with the university alumni association, which was continuing to withhold official recognition of GALA as a legitimate affinity group. After my first session, when I talked about life as an openly gay student at Notre Dame in the early 1980s, I decided to keep coming back. I wanted to get more engaged in advocating for LGBTQ inclusion at Notre Dame. Because I didn't want to disrupt the lives of Michael and our children anymore, I made the trip to South Bend alone. It provided a needed opportunity for prayer and grounding. Between attending Mass at the Basilica of the Sacred Heart and praying the rosary at the Grotto (of Our Lady of Lourdes) that weekend, I found new peace and strength for what would lie ahead in the coming weeks.

When I got back to Louisville, another family task arose. My three brothers and I wanted to organize a gathering with our families to celebrate our parents' sixty-seventh wedding anniversary. It would be an informal dinner at the U of L Hall of Fame Restaurant. By then, every year my parents had left together was a major milestone, so we made efforts to get the whole family together to celebrate. We didn't know it then, but it would be their last anniversary. My father passed the following January.

My parents liked going to that restaurant, perhaps because my father went to U of L night school many years after returning from World War II and had a great affinity for the school. I was also a graduate of U of L and was fortunate to have been one of the founding members of its LGBT Alumni Council in 2013, one of the first such official alumni councils at a southern university.

That June I was organizing the Lourdes Boy Scout troop's annual trip to summer camp for the second week of July and working as an Eagle Project coach with one of my favorite Scouts. It was also Pride Month, and the Louisville Pride Parade and Festival was taking place mid-month. The organizer of the parade, Kentuckiana Pride, had asked all the Kentucky marriage equality plaintiffs to be grand marshals for the event. We all jumped at the opportunity to get back together one more time to share a collective hug before we all faced the Court decision yet to be handed down. We were joined by the Kentucky legal team. In matching blue T-shirts that said "Paving the Way," we wanted to highlight the significance of the case for our state. It was one final opportunity for the plaintiffs and attorneys to get together and give each other a little encouragement as our time drew near.

In mid-June, I received an email that was also sent to the entire Freedom to Marry distribution list from Marc Solomon. He let everyone know that the Supreme Court could rule any day, with three possible outcomes:

1. The Court could give the freedom to marry nationwide by ruling that marriage bans are unconstitutional.
2. The Court could rule that nonmarriage states must respect marriages legally performed elsewhere, but that those states can keep in place their discriminatory bans.
3. The Court could rule that marriage bans do not violate the Constitution and that nonmarriage states do not have to respect the legal marriages of same-sex couples.

Of course, we were hoping for option 1. It would have the broadest effect by providing marriage equality for the whole country. At the very least, option 2 would allow people such as Michael and me, who'd married in other legal jurisdictions, to have our marriages recognized in our home state. Option 3 was certainly a possibility, though. We felt fear and concern over that dreadful prospect.

So many times before decision day, reporters asked family, co-workers, and friends what it would mean if we lost the case. That possibility was so grim that it was difficult to think about or talk about. We had to stiffen our resolve and discuss the many people whose lives would be negatively affected by that ruling. It was a big responsibility, a heavy weight that all the plaintiffs bore during this waiting period.

All the vested parties in the decision were moving forward with the assumption the Supreme Court would release its decision on Monday, June 29, so the ACLU made travel arrangements to have the four members of our family flown to DC on June 28. In the days leading up to departure we started receiving emails from James Esseks on travel and other details. James assured us that line-standers had been secured for us so we would have a place in the courtroom. Things were getting crazy, but it was all manageable.

ACLU undertook considerable coordination, planning, and assistance. I don't know how we would have managed decision day without its assistance. Everyone was still speculating the Court would rule on the 29th, but it could announce earlier. At the urging of the Human Rights Campaign, Jim Obergefell stayed at the ready in DC for the entire month of June just in case the Court made a surprise move and announced its decision before the 29th.

At work on Wednesday, June 24, I recall trolling the SCOTUSblog, which tracks live developments inside the Supreme Court. Although possible but not expected, I wanted to see if our case was called for that day. At the same time I was monitoring the blog, I was instant messaging a gay co-worker of mine, Paul Zielberg, who was doing precisely the same thing. Would this be the day? What would we do? What if the Court adds additional days to its session to release decisions? So many concerns were running through our minds. It was good to be able to share that experience with a supportive friend and fellow worker. As it turned out, the Court didn't call the *Obergefell* case that day, but it was adding an extra day to its calendar: Friday June 26.

Responding on the SCOTUSblog, which is interactive, one person asked, "Do you think that adding June 26th to the calendar for orders/opinions could be intended to coincide with the 2yr anniversary of DOMA being struck down, and the realization of SSM [same-sex marriage] Nationwide? It has me a bit optimistic, but not getting my hopes up just yet."[20] Before then, I hadn't really thought about that at all, but the possibility was intriguing. But then I realized that if the decision did come down that day, our family would miss being in DC because we weren't due to fly out until Sunday. Happily, nearly everyone on the blog said no, it was going to be on the last day because the *Obergefell* case was argued so late in the session.

That relief was shattered later that afternoon after the day's Court session ended. The ACLU believed that, because of the addition of Friday the 26th to the Court's calendar, and based on undisclosed inside intelligence, decision day was probably going to be that Friday the 26th. We were asked by the ACLU to drop everything, pack bags, and get on a flight the next day (Thursday) so we could be in the SCOTUS courtroom on Friday morning.

That was an abrupt, unexpected, big ask. Michael and I had busy corporate work lives with packed schedules, and our children had busy teenage schedules with work and other commitments. Still, we knew this

---

20. Kali Borkowski, "Live blog of opinions | June 26, 2015," SCOTUSblog, June 24, 2015, https://www.scotusblog.com/2015/06/live-blog-of-opinions-16/.

was one of those tough life decisions to make, like filing our case in the first place. Our family was all-in. I dropped everything at work and got approval from my manager to be out the rest of the week. The family assembled at home to pack and make arrangements to clear our calendars so we could get out of town the next day. Thank God for small favors, at least the children were out of school for summer break and we didn't have to secure special school absence permissions.

A flight from Louisville was not available until later the next day. Thunderstorms delayed our flight, and while waiting in Louisville we received a message from James Esseks that line-standers had been secured so we could get into the courtroom the next day. The only problem: we had to be in front of the Supreme Court by 7 a.m. Friday.

Our flight arrived late at Ronald Reagan Washington National Airport, and we were very tired when we checked into our hotel. We told the children to get to bed right away because we all had to be up well before dawn. That night was a bit of a challenge. We could barely get any sleep. All we could think about was what might happen, for better or worse, the next day.

Assistant Scoutmaster Greg Bourke and his son, Isaiah De Leon, at Isaiah's October 2013 Eagle Court of Honor. Photo credit: Andy Lyons.

Honorees for 2013 *Out* 100. From left: Greg Bourke, Dave Knapp, and Pascal Tessier, representing three generations of scouters discriminated against by the Boy Scouts of America, August 2013. Photo credit: Danielle Levitt. @daniel leleviG.

Bourke De Leon family outside the U.S. Supreme Court Building, June 2016. From left: Greg, Bryson, Isaiah, and Michael. Photo credit: Judy Rolfe, Rolfe Media. ©JudyRolfe.

Greg Bourke and Michael De Leon at the U.S. Supreme Court, June 2016.
Photo credit: Judy Rolfe, Rolfe Media. ©JudyRolfe.

Bourke De Leon family at Human Rights Campaign headquarters in Washington, DC, for the one-year anniversary of the *Obergefell* decision, June 2016. From left: Michael, Bryson, Greg, and Isaiah. Photo credit: Judy Rolfe, Rolfe Media. ©JudyRolfe.

The thirty-seven plaintiffs and numerous attorneys from four states involved in *Obergefell v. Hodges*, outside the Supreme Court Building on the night before oral arguments, April 27, 2015. Photo credit: Molly Kaplan, ©ACLU.

Isaiah De Leon answers anti–marriage equality protestors by defiantly march-ing past them with the Pride flag on the night before oral arguments, April 27, 2015. Photo credit: Molly Kaplan, ©ACLU.

A lighter moment with some of the *Obergefell* plaintiffs on the Supreme Court steps the day before oral arguments, April 27, 2015. Photo credit: Molly Kaplan, ©ACLU.

The jubilant crowd celebrates the 5–4 SCOTUS decision for marriage equality on the Supreme Court Plaza on decision day, June 26, 2015. Photo credit: Molly Kaplan, ©ACLU.

Victorious attorneys Doug Hallward-Driemeier (*left*) and Mary Bounato (*right*) flanking James Esseks of the ACLU addressing the crowd after the decision, June 26, 2015. Photo credit: Molly Kaplan, ©ACLU.

Named plaintiff Jim Obergefell addressing the crowd after the decision, June 26, 2015. Photo credit: Molly Kaplan, ©ACLU.

Plaintiffs Michael De Leon (*left*) and Greg Bourke (*right*) speaking after the decision, June 26, 2015. Photo credit: Molly Kaplan, ©ACLU.

Plaintiffs and attorneys rally after the decision, June 26, 2015. Photo credit: Molly Kaplan, ©ACLU.

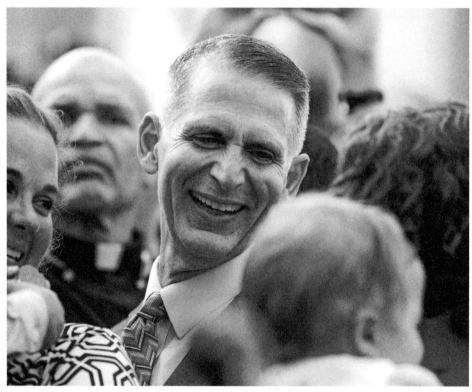

The sheer joy and relief of winning a U.S. Supreme Court case recognizing nationwide marriage equality. Greg Bourke on June 26, 2015. Photo credit: Molly Kaplan, ©ACLU.

Greg and Michael appearing on *Meet The Press* with attorney Mary Bounato (*left*) and host Chuck Todd (*right*) shortly after the SCOTUS marriage equality decision, June 26, 2015. Photo credit: Bryson De Leon.

The Bourke/De Leon family rallies outside the Supreme Court before oral arguments, April 28, 2015. From left: Isaiah, Bryson, Michael, and Greg. Photo credit: Barbara Proud.

25

MARRIAGE
EQUALITY DAY

Michael and I have always been early risers, often before 5 a.m., but after just a few hours of sleep we were up extra early the next morning to get shaved and showered. More importantly, we had to iron all the dress clothes for the four of us. We were amazed when we texted the kids in the next room that morning that they were also up and moving. That was perhaps one of my biggest concerns of the day.

We caught a taxi outside the hotel and arrived at the steps of the Supreme Court Building about 6:50 a.m. There was already a crowd and a lot of buzz. Frantically we searched for James Esseks because the line-standers were expecting to be relieved by 7 a.m. After we found him with just a few minutes to spare, the ACLU took some quick pictures of our family in front of the building holding an ACLU flag to use on social media. Then James led us to our spot in line.

It was still quite early, so we spent a lot of time chatting with others. Jim Obergefell was just ahead of us, so we took some pictures together and talked our way through some jitters. Also in line was *Washington Post* columnist Debbie Cenziper, who was gathering information for that book she was writing with Jim. Debbie ended up spending a lot of time with us, asking questions and taking notes. Besides us and Jim, the only other plaintiffs there were Pam and Nicole Yorksmith from Ohio, who were with their two young children. Tevin, one of Paul Campion and Randy Johnson's children, was supposed to arrive early that morning, but his flight was delayed. Unfortunately he didn't arrive in time to be seated in the courtroom.

After we stood in the queue outside for what seemed like an eternity, the line started moving into the Supreme Court Building and through the various security checkpoints. After finally getting inside, we still had a lot of time to kill, so we were escorted to the cafeteria to hang out and get breakfast. During oral arguments months earlier, our children had to wait in the cafeteria. This time they were excited to actually be going into the courtroom for the proceedings.

After I entered the food service area to get a cup of coffee, I turned around, looked up, and nearly ran into Justice Elena Kagan. We were both a little startled and stopped in our tracks to make lengthy eye contact. I said gently, "Excuse me." She gave me her big smile but said nothing. Obviously, I recognized her, and I sensed she knew who I was. Her wordless smile spoke volumes to me. I thought to myself, she knows what's going to happen today, and I wondered if that was her way of telling me that things were going to be all right.

After a quick breakfast, we were taken into a hallway outside the cafeteria. Just like on the day of oral arguments, we were moved in progression from one holding station to the next until we passed through the final security check. Putting cell phones into the lockers was the last step. Then we lined up outside those huge majestic entry doors. When summoned, we entered the courtroom and moved down the aisle. Fortunately, the four of us were able to sit together in a center aisle not far from the front. Security was once again very tight with numerous black suits about the room. The audience was again cautioned that no outbursts would be permitted. I asked myself, how was that supposed to work? Win or lose, how do you sit there unable to express your emotion after a truly historic decision gets announced? How could that possibly be done?

There was no guarantee the *Obergefell* case would be decided that morning, so we could have been setting ourselves up for just a few hours listening to tedious legal opinions on other cases about which we had no concern. But somehow we felt it was going to be our day.

After settling into our seats, we girded ourselves for the possibility the ruling wouldn't be read. Maybe we'd have to listen to another decision before *Obergefell v. Hodges* was called. The justices entered, took their seats, and called our case right away—it was quite startling. My first thought was that I wasn't ready for this. Why couldn't we hear another decision first? Michael and I looked at each other and reached for each other's hand. The moment of truth was finally upon us.

The clerk announced Justice Anthony Kennedy. He would be reading the majority opinion. At that precise moment we knew we'd won. Kennedy had authored and delivered the majority decision for the *Windsor* case. We knew right then we'd secured the five votes needed to get the decision we were seeking. I looked at Michael and whispered, "We won." We squeezed each other's hands gently. That was about as much celebration as we were allowed in that moment. As we looked around the courtroom, we saw people choking back tears, covering their mouths, expressing muffled and silent joy. There was so much relief after so many years of pent-up frustration. It was a remarkable feeling and one that was then heightened considerably by Kennedy's magnificent reading.

Justice Kennedy was joined in his opinion by Justices Ginsburg, Breyer, Sotomayor, and Kagan. The majority opinion was a masterpiece, one that we very much appreciated hearing spoken live. I've read it several times since them. Each time I read it, it seems more powerful and moving.

Kennedy provided numerous legal arguments for the decision. For example, he noted that autonomy and making free personal choices are guaranteed under the Fourteenth Amendment. So is the fact that marriage constitutes an agreement unlike any other to allow unique commitment between two individuals. He stated: "Far from seeking to devalue marriage, the petitioners seek it for themselves because of their respect—and need—for its privileges and responsibilities. And their immutable nature dictates that same-sex marriage is their only real path to this profound commitment."[21]

The point in his opinion that resonated most powerfully for our family was that marriage "safeguards children and families and thus

---

21. *Obergefell v. Hodges* decision: Supreme Court of the United States, "576 U.S. (2015) 1 Opinion of the Court, JAMES OBERGEFELL, ET AL., PETITIONERS 14–556 v. RICHARD HODGES, DIRECTOR, OHIO DEPARTMENT OF HEALTH, ET AL.," June 26, 2015, pp. 1, 9, https://www.supremecourt.gov/opinions/14pdf/14-556_3204.pdf.

draws meaning from related rights of childrearing, procreation, and education."[22]

As we sat there, I thought about the seventeen years I'd raised our children without a legal relationship to them. How much anxiety that lack of legality had caused us. This was the reason we decided to pursue this lawsuit in the first place. Our family and others like ours needed and deserved the same safeguards and legal protections that other families with married parents enjoyed. Kennedy's words were the most satisfying moment in the midst of a monumentally bigger experience.

While Kennedy continued to read, I kept scanning the justices to see how they were reacting. For the most part they were all pretty stone-faced, as you might expect. But every time I looked at Justice Sotomayor she was staring right at our family. You know how you can tell when someone is looking at you. It was obvious she was watching us for our reactions. Michael and I couldn't talk about it then, but later that day Michael told me he also noticed precisely the same thing: Sotomayor's unwavering stare. Was it because Michael and she shared Hispanic heritage? Was it the fact we were all devout Catholics? Or did we simply present one unique face of family diversity 2015 style? It wasn't a creepy or intimidating stare. It felt more like that of a loving mother watching over her children. She seemed to be conveying a sense of don't worry, I'm taking care of you.

The capstone of Justice Kennedy's majority opinion was a beauty. It was a powerful statement which since that day has become more meaningful to me every time I hear it read as vows at same-sex marriages:

No union is more profound than marriage, for it embodies the highest ideals of love, fidelity, devotion, sacrifice, and family. In forming a marital union, two people become something greater than once they were. As some of the petitioners in these cases demonstrate, marriage embodies a love that may endure even past death. It would misunderstand these men and women to say they disrespect the idea of marriage. Their plea is that they do respect it, respect it so deeply that they seek to find its fulfillment for themselves. Their hope is not to be condemned to live in loneliness, excluded from one of civiliza-

22. *Obergefell v. Hodges*, 19.

tion's oldest institutions. They ask for equal dignity in the eyes of the law. The Constitution grants them that right.[23]

Well, what do you do after that? You still have to sit and listen to the dissenting opinion that was delivered in this case by Chief Justice Roberts. He was joined by Justices Scalia and Thomas. The Roberts's dissent was particularly irritating because when we went into the courtroom, we thought he'd been enough of a centrist to cast his vote on the right side of history. When he chose to vote against this liberty and deliver a scathing opinion against it, my personal opinion of him diminished considerably.

Roberts hit that old sour note again. This change, he decided, should not happen through the Court but through legislative means or the votes of constituents: that horrendously long game of winning hearts and minds. His closing remarks were particularly irritating: "If you are among the many Americans—of whatever sexual orientation—who favor expanding same-sex marriage, by all means celebrate today's decision. Celebrate the achievement of a desired goal. Celebrate the opportunity for a new expression of commitment to a partner. Celebrate the availability of new benefits. But do not celebrate the Constitution. It had nothing to do with it."[24]

After a few more formalities, the justices and courtroom audience were abruptly dismissed. Finally, Michael and I were able to stand up and share a celebratory hug and a kiss on the way out the door. As those in attendance moved out of the courtroom, the mood enlivened. It seemed everyone was in a triumphant mood. I'm sure there were some in the room who'd been hoping for the opposite decision, but they couldn't be readily identified. The joy seemed to be spreading universally. The euphoria couldn't be contained.

After we retrieved our cell phones from the lockers and prepared to exit the front doors, we anticipated that long walk down the iconic front steps to face the crowd waiting to greet us. As we moved toward the door, security stopped us. The door was blocked. They told us we had to exit through the inner stairs and out the side door, then walk around the building to the plaza in front. Why? we asked. They didn't tell us. There was some chattering about a bomb threat outside and they needed to

---

23. *Obergefell v. Hodges*, 33.
24. *Obergefell v. Hodges*, 68.

keep the area clear. Joy briefly turned to fear as we considered the possibility that some disturbed individual might resort to mass violence. That wasn't going to stop us from exiting.

We saw Jim Obergefell with his attorney, Al Gerhardstein, hurrying toward the inner stairs to find the way out. We had caught up with James Esseks from the ACLU and followed Al and Jim through the building and out the side door. It wasn't the exit we were anticipating. There was no one there to greet us. By that point Pam and Nicole Yorksmith and their kids had caught up with us as we walked briskly toward the front plaza. We finally learned there hadn't been a bomb threat. Instead, when the huge crowd outside heard the decision, it had stormed the steps. Security had to shut down the upper plaza and restore order.

Finally, the group of plaintiffs and attorneys turned the corner and we could start to see the crowd. It was so much bigger than expected. It had grown exponentially during the morning while we were inside. When Jim, Pam and Nicole, and Michael and I walked through the crowd with some of our attorneys, we were greeted like conquering heroes. Slaps on the back and random side hugs from strangers came from all directions as we tried to walk through the crowd to get to the podium to address the substantial gathering of media that was waiting. People often ask what that experience was like. I just tell them it was like winning the Gay Super Bowl. We felt like the champions of the world for one brief moment. But the most satisfaction came from simply winning. Our family and other families like ours were finally safe. Love won.

The plaintiffs and attorneys took turns speaking to the media and the eager crowd. Of course, Jim did a splendid job, as did Mary Bonauto and Doug Hallward-Driemeier, the attorneys who spoke on our behalf at oral arguments. This time I was actually prepared to speak and had a coherent set of talking points. I don't think anybody cared much about what any of us were saying specifically. Mostly they just wanted to hear the victory speeches after waiting so long for marriage equality.

After the speeches were done, we broke into smaller groups to address the different clusters of media set up for interviews. We went through so many interviews that day, I lost track of whom we were talking to and even what was being said. The highlight came as we were standing next to Jim Obergefell. President Obama was calling Jim's cell phone to congratulate him on the decision. By that point Tevin Johnson-Campion had finally arrived. It was nice to have another Kentucky plaintiff join in addressing the media.

It was a hot day in Washington, DC, and we were all wearing business suits, so we were baking, but we just didn't care. We would have stood there all day to revel in the victory, but it wasn't just our victory. It was a victory for every person celebrating there. Our joy was both communal and intensely personal.

Since then, many LGBTQ people throughout the country have told me they remember exactly where they were and what they were doing when they heard about the decision. I tell them that we older folks all remember where and when we heard the news that President Kennedy was shot. This decision seems to have been a similar type of event for LGBTQ people because so many people have shared their personal stories of that moment with us.

Eventually the ACLU representatives, Steve Smith, Diana Scholl, James Esseks, and Crystal Cooper, gathered up the Kentucky plaintiffs and took us to a war room in the next block so we could participate in additional phone interviews. More importantly, Diana arranged to get us some much-needed lunch from the Supreme Court cafeteria. We sat there with the ACLU contingent as we ate lunch and took calls and talked about what might happen the rest of the day.

26

MEET THE PRESS

Late in the afternoon, Crystal Cooper took us to a studio to do a live interview. They'd arranged a car to get there. By that point I was so tired I didn't even know or care where we were going, but I dutifully got in and we zipped through downtown DC to a destination I did not know to speak with someone I also did not know. On the way, Bryson received a call from a former grade-school classmate who was working on an article about the decision for her high school newspaper. It was the strangest sensation to hear him being interviewed in the car. Everything that was happening seemed surreal.

Our destination ended up being an NBC studio. We learned that the interview was to be with Chuck Todd for a pre-recorded segment of a *Meet the Press* that included Mary Bonauto. They shuffled us into the studio and led us back to makeup. After all that time sweating in the sun while talking to the media, a little freshening up was necessary. As we and Mary were going through the preparations, Chuck Todd walked in and started hanging out with us. He asked about the case and the decision, of course, but then we moved on to talking politics in general. Of course, politics was Chuck's expertise. It was mind-blowing that we were actually just hanging out with him, talking politics, while waiting to go on *Meet the Press*.

When the show started taping, Mary did most of the talking. She was the legal expert and should have been the one to explain it from that perspective. Michael and I did get to make several key points, particularly how important it was to win at the U.S. Supreme Court because that was the only practical way it was going to happen in Kentucky in our lifetimes. We pointed out how Kentucky is often resistant to change on progressive social issues like this. Fully 75 percent of Kentuckians voting in 2004 had endorsed the state constitutional amendment banning same-sex marriage—just eleven years earlier. There was a strong turnout for Kentucky elections for that vote, with 54 percent of all registered voting on the amendment. That reflected interest not only in the presidential and Senate/House candidates but also conservative voters wanting to make a statement on the amendment. Opinions and times were changing in Kentucky, but at a snail's pace, so justice required the Supreme Court to step in. When the taping was over, we took some keepsake pictures on the set with Chuck Todd and Mary, and got souvenir *Meet the Press* coffee mugs.

It was already early evening when we were wrapping things up at the studio. Given that we had gotten up well before 5 a.m. to get to court by 7 a.m., it had been a long and exhausting day. After saying farewell to the ACLU representatives, we returned to the hotel so we could seek out some dinner. As we ate, our family thought about heading back over to the Supreme Court Building after dinner to see if there were any revelers left that we could join, but everyone was simply too exhausted for any more excitement that day.

27

NEW YORK PRIDE

While in the hotel room that night, we emailed Crystal Cooper to ask if instead of ACLU getting us a flight back to Louisville, could we take the train to New York City the next day (Saturday) to participate in the New York Pride March on Sunday. I had marched in the honor guard there with Scouts for Equality the previous two years, but I didn't sign up for the 2015 event because I assumed we'd be stuck in DC waiting for the ruling on Monday. With the decision coming on Friday, we were free. The thought of having the Bourke De Leon family participate in the New York Pride March was very appealing right about then. The ACLU national offices were in New York, so they agreed. They thought it would provide great visibility to have us join the Pride March. The next morning the Bourke De Leon family boarded an Amtrak train from DC to New York. Our kids called it the "Victory Train."

On the train, I was messaging with several of my Scouts for Equality mates to let them know I was going to be there to march with the group behind the honor guard. Because I was not planning on coming to New York, I hadn't packed my Scout uniform for the trip. Without the uniform I could not march in the front carrying flags in the honor guard. When my scouter friends Crystal Bueno, Stacie Sarnicola, and Mark Noel heard that, they sprang into action and pulled together a uniform I could use. They thoughtfully purchased a Scout uniform shirt, bought all the appropriate badges, and sewed them on so I would be prepared to march.

The New York Pride March that year was an exuberant celebration of the nationwide marriage equality decision, so it seemed fitting that I managed to get the opportunity to march in the honor guard that day with the Boy Scouts.

On Sunday morning, we got up early again, tired from all the excitement and travel of the last few days. But duty called. Two friends and fellow plaintiffs from the *Obergefell* case, Joe Vitale and Rob Talmas, lived in New York, so we agreed to meet them at an early morning pre-march breakfast at a local pub. Joe and Rob had adopted an infant in Ohio. That was how they came to be Ohio plaintiffs in *Obergefell*. They'd sought to have both their names listed on the adopted child's birth certificate. Their story was so similar to ours that we all became quick friends. As we gathered at the pub with many of their friends from the New York marriage equality movement, joy was in the air. Maybe it was because it was Pride March day, but everybody was also buzzing about the Supreme Court marriage equality ruling. There seemed to be a sense of euphoria and relief everywhere.

Before the march, a kickoff program took place at the march registration area. Scouts for Equality founder Zach Wahls and I were asked to speak to the crowd. While waiting, our family huddled with other speakers, including Sir Ian McKellen and Sir Derek Jacobi. Our teenage children were beside themselves. They actually got to meet and hang out with Magneto, McKellen's character in the wildly popular X-Men movies. When it was my turn to speak to the crowd, I mentioned that our family was in New York to take a victory lap, but the next day we'd be returning to semihostile Kentucky, the home of Mitch McConnell, Rand Paul, and the vast population of people who opposed our efforts to bring marriage equality to the commonwealth. That moment in New York was sweet, but we knew the climate back home would not be so welcoming.

When it came time to line up for the honor guard, Michael and I were reunited with many of our Scouts for Equality friends, including my *Out* 100 co-honorees, Dave Knapp and Pascal Tessier, who joined in the honor guard. Michael and our children marched with the group just behind the flag line and the Scouts for Equality banner. Having done this for the two previous years in New York, we could tell there was a particularly large Scouts for Equality group in attendance that year—Scout participation in the event had grown each year.

Marching in an honor guard is not like riding on a float, smiling and continuously waving to the crowd. It requires using both hands on a very long flagpole that is seated around the waist in a neck harness. It makes waving to the crowd nearly impossible. Further, the honor guard has to keep the flags at the proper angle, pay close attention to maintain correct spacing between the other flag bearers, and attempt to keep in step with the flag line. This requires physical exertion and mental concentration to produce a respectable looking honor guard for that very long Pride March route. Still, glancing to the left and the right, I managed to absorb plenty of the joy and celebration as we marched through those packed Manhattan streets. As the honor guard does every year, when we passed the famous Stonewall Inn, we stopped and pivoted to face it and deliver a coordinated scout salute.

When we reached the end of the route, we took an annual Scouts for Equality group photo. Many of us then went out for a Scout lunch. To complete the day, we visited the Pride Street Fair in Greenwich Village. Again, all the buzz was over marriage equality. By the end of the day we had walked many miles, and the Bourke De Leon family was exhausted. We were more than ready to head back home to Kentucky and get back into our everyday lives. The day before when we were heading to New York, I had tried to set up a spur-of-the-moment meeting with Edie Windsor on the day of the Pride March. That didn't work out, but after I returned home I received an email on my computer:

> Dear Greg and Michael: I'm so sorry I missed you. I haven't been well so I didn't go in but watched from the judge's table (where the parade turned from 5th avenue onto 8th st. . . . I'm so happy for you that the ordeal is over and that you won. Send my love to your teenagers.
> Thank you so much for thinking of me.
> Love to all of you.
> Edie

How incredibly fortunate we were to have had the opportunity to know and draw inspiration from someone who had such a profound effect on LGBTQ history.

Back home in Kentucky, the local victory party with the other Kentucky plaintiffs and attorneys had already taken place. On decision day the Fairness Campaign gave recognition to the Kentucky plaintiffs. Local progressive politicians such as our U.S. rep John Yarmuth, Louisville mayor Greg Fischer, and quite a few other state and local officials offered congratulations. Several additional events were being planned to celebrate the victory. Michael and I were happy to reunite with the other plaintiffs and attorneys to express gratitude for the support we got from elected officials and the general public.

A couple of weeks after the ruling, Evan Wolfson and his Freedom to Marry organization planned another celebration. Even before the decision was announced, Evan had sent out invitations in early June to save the date of July 9, win or lose at the Supreme Court. Michael and I had planned to attend all along, but since we'd just returned from New York Pride, we weren't thrilled about going right back to New York City.

The Freedom to Marry celebration took place at the Cipriani Wall Street. It ended up being a star-studded event with great entertainment and a keynote address by Vice President Joe Biden, a longtime supporter of LGBTQ rights. All the *Obergefell* plaintiffs had been invited along with many of those who had been marriage equality plaintiffs in other states over the years. That evening we settled in with fellow *Obergefell* plaintiffs Ijpe DeKoe and Thom Kostura from the Tennessee case. We spent most of the evening talking about the BSA and its ongoing refusal to admit gay leaders. Thom and Ijpe had met as young adults in 1999 when they were both working at a Boy Scout summer camp in Rhode Island. They'd risen to become Eagle Scouts. Thom and Ijpe shared my passion for working to eliminate discrimination in the BSA, but eventually we all decided that night was more about celebrating the marriage equality victory. It was absolutely an evening to remember.

After we returned to Louisville, we had one last victory celebration a few days later with several attorneys, including Mary Bonauto, Jeffrey Fisher, and James Esseks. Representative Yarmuth and Mayor Fischer also showed up to say a few words and express gratitude for the efforts of all the attorneys and plaintiffs. After an eventful couple of weeks, we really were quite ready for life to get back to normal.

28

BACK TO WORK SCOUTING FOR EQUALITY

Very quickly the dust settled, and Michael and I returned to our challenging corporate jobs. We'd missed several work days for the DC and New York trips, but duty called at the office. We quickly found ourselves consumed with the regular day-to-day work grind. With marriage equality behind us, and after visiting in New York with the Scouts for Equality crew, I suddenly felt reenergized to resume working toward getting the BSA to drop its ban on lesbian and gay leaders. I started working again with Zach Wahls, Eric Andresen, and others to strategize our next steps. With marriage equality now the law of the land, there was new enthusiasm for pursuing other LGBTQ rights. Having already been a victim of BSA discrimination, I knew where I wanted to concentrate my efforts.

Before the marriage equality decision, I'd been working with attorneys Shannon Fauver and Dawn Elliott to possibly launch a lawsuit against the BSA based on age discrimination. It did not make sense to me that in 2015 a youth member in Boy Scouts could be openly gay until age eighteen, but openly gay people eighteen and older were prohibited from membership. The attorneys were researching all the angles, but they'd discouraged me from doing anything until after the marriage equality case fully played out.

Before we got very far along developing a case, something unexpected and wonderful occurred. On July 13, 2015, the BSA abruptly announced that its National Executive Board would meet on July 27 to ratify a resolution to end its ban on gay Scout leaders. The new proposal would allow sponsoring organizations of Scout units to select their leaders. The national organization would not enforce a mandatory membership ban based on sexual orientation. This was widely seen as a response to BSA president Robert Gates's call to completely end the ban, but it didn't go quite that far.

The proposed arrangement would let sponsoring organizations set their own membership policies, but those organizations could (and likely would) still continue to ban gay leaders. Since 70 percent of BSA units in the United States were sponsored by churches, this was a concern. We knew that these sponsoring organizations were being given a license to discriminate.

The BSA could have taken a more forceful position, as it did with the youth membership policy revision. It could have chosen to forbid all LGBTQ discrimination in membership regardless of age. But it was creating a two-path membership policy, and this was not going to satisfy many of its critics on either side of the argument.

The local media wanted my take on this anticipated change. I was obliged to share my disappointment with them. Joe Sonka, a reporter with a local online publication called *Insider Louisville*, contacted me on July 16, 2015, for comment. He shared with me a response he'd received from the Archdiocese of Louisville:

> The Archdiocese does not set the policies for the Boy Scouts; however we can set policies for troops that are sponsored by parishes. In light of the anticipated change on the national level, this issue will be discussed with the Catholic Committee on Scouting in the near future.
>
> However, our general expectation is that adult leaders—whether heterosexual or with same-sex attraction—in a Church-sponsored youth activity (including Boy Scouts) strive to lead chaste lives and seek to both accept and witness to the full teaching of the Church on chastity and charity, including teachings on the sanctity of marriage. This is consistent with our expectation of all pastoral leaders.

Cecelia Hart Price
Chief Communications Officer
Archdiocese of Louisville

This response was expected. The policy change would certainly be a cause for concern to the Archdiocese, because before this the BSA was the bad guy in this controversy and took all the heat over its discriminatory membership policy. Now the sponsoring organizations were going to have to be the ones to make and create inequitable policies and take the blame for discriminating against gay and lesbian leaders. The Catholic Church still refused to recognize my marriage, so I could certainly never meet its standards to be a Scout leader. Does the Church apply these same criteria to any other group in excluding them from participation? It would be a pretty clear policy of antigay discrimination. The Archdiocese appeared to be putting the policy in place largely to retaliate for the Church's stinging setback with the same-sex marriage issue.

While I dealt with this challenge, inspiration came to me to write another letter to the Reverend John Jenkins, president of the University of Notre Dame, to appeal for official recognition of the gay and lesbian alumni group GALA. Just after the *Obergefell* decision, there was a great groundswell of support for LGBTQ rights and what seemed to be a leap forward for inclusion. Optimistic that the time might be right to make another request of Reverend Jenkins, I poured my heart out in a personal letter passionately requesting GALA recognition. Jenkins quickly responded on July 15, 2015:

Dear Greg

Thank you for your letter of July 12 and for returning to our recent Reunion Weekend. It was very gratifying to hear of your current life, your spouse and children and your wonderful family. I will pray for God's continued blessings on you and those that are dear to you.

I appreciate your reflections on Notre Dame and what we might do to be more supportive of LGBT members of our community, and I am sorry to hear that some think we have not done enough. As you point out in your letter, we have made steps recently to support our undergraduate LGBT community and we will continue to work on these and other initiatives. We remain a Catholic university, as I am sure that you know, and we will also continue to work with the wider Church in thinking with our tradition on these challenging issues and striving to understand God's will for you. I would humbly ask the same respect for us and others in the Church as we strive to discern God's will.

Thank you for writing. We are proud to call you a graduate of Notre Dame. Please know that you are and will remain in my prayers, and I ask for your prayers for me.

In Notre Dame,

Rev. John L. Jenkins, C.S.C.

President

After I read these compassionate words from Reverend Jenkins, my spirit soared. Growing up in an Irish Catholic working-class family, I never received a lot of strokes or proud-of-you moments, instead it seemed there was primarily criticism, guilt, and disappointment. For the president of Our Lady's university to make such a statement pumped me up more than he possibly could have imagined. To my knowledge, absolutely nothing changed at Notre Dame as a result of my letter, or at least nothing tangible that could be seen or touched. But it felt like a great success. I'd started what seemed to be a meaningful dialogue with someone deeply respected and who had the capacity to ultimately change things and create a more diverse and inclusive Notre Dame.

As the July 23 date approached for the anticipated BSA vote on changing its adult membership policy, Scouts for Equality mobilized its media response team. Those who would be addressing the media were provided with Scouts for Equality talking points regarding the membership change. Justin Wilson at Scouts for Equality provided to me a media list for my region. After the vote, media volunteers were going to release statements to local and statewide outlets to make ourselves available for comments. Zach Wahls also contacted me and said to expect direct contact from national media because of my history with both the BSA and the marriage equality decision.

As expected, the BSA Executive Board voted to end its long-standing ban on openly gay and lesbian leaders with a resounding 79 percent vote in favor of the change. But in its announcement the BSA pointed out that units sponsored by religious chartered organizations would continue to use "religious beliefs" as criteria for selecting leaders.

Most people in the Scouts for Equality realm thought any movement was a good thing. But everyone acknowledged that certain religious groups that sponsor large numbers of Scout units, such as the Church of Latter-Day Saints and the Catholic Church, would continue to prevent openly lesbian and gay leaders from serving. This presented a bit of a challenge when we talked to the media. We had to stick to the Scouts for Equality talking points about the significance of any change in this direction while tempering concern it would mean no practical change at all for people like me.

Seth Adam from GLAAD reached out to ask about doing a couple of national media spots the next day, one in the morning with CNN and one in the afternoon with Thomas Roberts on MSNBC. By this point I was really weary of dealing with the media, but I felt it important to show up and raise awareness about this good news/bad news development.

The interview with Thomas Roberts was particularly productive because he quickly grasped the issue. He understood there would be no change for people like me who wanted to serve as a leader in a unit sponsored by certain churches. An openly gay man himself, Roberts was sympathetic to concerns about the limitations with the new BSA adult membership policy and asked relevant questions. But at the end of the interview he really threw me off with one question: Which Boy Scout merit badge, he asked, would I most like to serve on as counselor? It seemed off-topic. A little flustered, I responded Personal Management because it's often the last one that's completed by scouts because of the copious notetaking requirements. After finishing up that interview and a couple more radio segments, I was more than ready to get back to my day job in analytics at Humana Military Healthcare.

Later that day an unexpected email popped up from our former attorney from fifteen years ago. Karen Stewart had long since moved to Wisconsin. She'd done all the legal work for Michael and me after we adopted our children to put in place as many legal protections as possible, short of getting legally married. Karen said she just watched my interview with Roberts on MSNBC. The marriage equality ruling was still just a few weeks old, so she asked, "How does it feel to hit two out of the ball park in one summer?" That was sort of the prevailing feeling at that particular moment for the LGBTQ equality movement: taking down marriage inequality and finally getting the BSA to back off its total ban on gay leaders. But it was also evident to many that the battle with the BSA was far from over.

With the BSA's newly issued license to discriminate, the next obvious step for me was to check with the Archdiocese of Louisville to see if it would in fact continue to ban gay leaders from serving in troops that it sponsored. In an email to Cecelia Price, communication director at the Archdiocese of Louisville, I asked:

> Today I am seeking guidance from you about what the policy will be with our Church and within the Archdiocese of Louisville. If I re-apply to be an adult leader for Boy Scout Troop 325 at Our Lady of Lourdes, will the Archdiocese approve my application for membership?
>
> Further, if the Archdiocese imposes a ban on gay/lesbian adults from participating as adult leaders in its sponsored Boy Scout units, will it also impose this ban for gay/lesbian leaders with Girl Scout units sponsored by the Archdiocese?
>
> I have been a registered Girl Scout leader at Lourdes for about ten years. If the Archdiocese is going to have a policy of banning gay and lesbian adult leaders within the Boy Scouts at its sponsored units, it should be consistent and do the same with its Girl Scout units.
>
> Please let me know what the policy will be going forward for adults serving in these ministries in units sponsored by Archdiocesan parishes.

Not surprisingly, I received no response, which was precisely what I expected. The Archdiocese did not like to go on record with controversial issues like this and would often avoid making any statement or committing anything to print. I and our local media sent follow-up requests on my behalf. They also went unreturned. I waited for some type of response.

Finally, on Monday, August 3, 2015, I got a phone call from my pastor's administrative assistant asking me to come into the parish center for a meeting with Father Scott the next morning. I had received a call like that once before to come in and talk to my pastor when the Lincoln Heritage Council was putting pressure on Father Scott to force me out of leadership three years earlier, so it was apparent what this new meeting request was about.

The next day I stopped by for the early morning appointment on my way to work. Father Scott greeted me warmly in the welcoming way one expects from their faith leader. We moved to his private office and closed the door. After a few moments of idle chit-chat, Father Scott informed me the Archdiocese had received my request, and he just said, "The answer is no."

Father Scott made it clear it was not his decision, that this was something out of his hands. I told him the news was disappointing but not surprising. I had been hopeful the world had changed enough that the Archdiocese might also change its position and let fairness prevail. We shook hands cordially and parted ways. At that point I realized I would most likely never be allowed to return to Scout leadership at my troop at Lourdes. As I left the parish center, I walked to my car and got in, indulged myself in a brief cry of disappointment, then started my car and drove to work.

That same day, Rachel Platt, a reporter at a local TV station, forwarded a note she'd obtained from the Archdiocese. It said a letter had been sent to all the local Catholic priests that week. It included this statement from the national Catholic Committee on Scouting:

STATEMENT. Our Scout troops are ministries of the parishes in which they reside. As a Church deeply committed to proper formation, we have both the right and the responsibility to choose leaders whose character and conduct are consistent with Church teaching. All pastoral leaders in these ministries should be able to provide a credible and integrated witness in their lives to the teachings of the Catholic Church, including its teachings on marriage, sexuality, and charity. The resolution passed by the Boy Scouts appears to respect the right of religious organizations to choose leaders based upon religious principles.

We begin with the assumption of good faith and character among volunteer ministers, and these volunteers are chosen and supervised on the parish level for parish ministries.
Archdiocese of Louisville
August 4, 2015

News of this announcement got out to the local media, and there was a considerable amount of outrage over the new policy, which would certainly enable antigay discrimination by the Church. Chris Hartman from the Fairness Campaign was particularly livid and started mobilizing his forces to launch an online shame campaign against Archbishop Kurtz. He also reviewed Archbishop Kurtz's schedule for an opportunity to catch him in public and organize a protest rally he couldn't escape. Still hurting and feeling a little immobilized from the rejection, I backed off and let Chris take the lead on making plans for a public response.

29

AN AUDIENCE WITH
THE ARCHBISHOP

Before the Archdiocesan policy was announced, Chris Hartman had made several attempts to set up a meeting with the chancellor for the Archdiocese of Louisville, Brian Reynolds, to talk about what the decision might be. Reynolds wouldn't return phone calls to Hartman and wouldn't agree to a meeting with Chris. Likewise, I had also tried to arrange a meeting at the Archdiocese before and after its Boy Scout policy announcement, but without success. When the local media pressed for answers about its decision, the Archdiocesan spokesperson, Cecelia Price, stated simply, "We do not discuss with the media the pastoral situation of individual parishioners."[25]

Forces had been mobilizing nationally to support me because of my rejection. Change.org was planning to launch a petition challenging the Archdiocese's decision. My contacts at Scouts for Equality, GLAAD, and ACLU national were preparing their own campaigns to challenge it. After about a week of stewing, I decided that, given all the media criticism of the Archdiocese and the external pressure, it might be worthwhile for me to make one more attempt to set up a meeting. With all the bad

---

25. Andy Wolfson, "Gay Scout Leader Rejected by Louisville Parish," *Courier-Journal*, August 4, 2015, https://www.courier-journal.com/story/news/local/2015/08/04/gay-scout-leader-rejected-louisville-parish/31136129/.

press the Archdiocese was receiving, I thought one of those pastoral discussions to cool things off might be appropriate. I sent an email to the Archdiocese on August 12. Two days later, Brian Reynolds informed me the Archbishop was open to meeting with me.

Nearly two weeks passed before he got back with proposed times for a meeting. He also suggested we invite Chris Hartman from the Fairness Campaign to join Archbishop Kurtz and him in the meeting. For some unknown reason there suddenly seemed a sense of urgency. He offered a meeting for Tuesday, August 25, at 3 p.m. at the Chancery. Chris and I arrived separately. As we sat in the lobby, I recalled the time I spent there in the Chancery working in the Stewardship and Development Office in 1999–2000. Nothing ever changed at the Chancery. It still looked and felt the same with its 1970s décor. At least I was in a very familiar place.

The great unknown was what, if any, new attacks the Archdiocese might be planning to launch on me at that meeting. It had already decided to take a hard line and prevent me or any other gay or lesbian person from serving as a leader in its Scout units, but would the Archdiocese take further moves? Would I be asked to leave the Church? Might they even excommunicate me? Would I be required to resign my position as a Girl Scout leader at Lourdes? Would I be forced to terminate my longtime service as a Communion minister at Lourdes? The Archdiocese had many options open for retaliation. As I sat there waiting, I feared the worst.

Reynolds finally appeared, greeted Chris and me, and escorted us into Archbishop Kurtz's office. It was a pleasant space with large, comfortable upholstered chairs. It was a cheery place, but the mood itself was somber and tense.

After shaking hands, Archbishop Kurtz started off by addressing the Boy Scouts' policy change. He suggested that the BSA had adopted a policy that allowed religious organizations to establish their own membership policies. Of course, he was technically correct. It was not prudent to argue with anything he was saying other than the fact I'd expressed disapproval of the new BSA policy. Archbishop Kurtz contended my service could not be allowed because I was not in compliance with Church teachings requiring me to remain chaste. Honestly, I was quite intimidated by Archbishop Kurtz. It was his office. He was in complete control of the situation. I found it extremely difficult to challenge him on the policy points he was making.

Chris Hartman was quite a bit more agitated and assertive. He criticized the Archdiocese for the long history of LGBTQ marginalization he'd witnessed over the years. Archbishop Kurtz and Reynolds never got rattled. They stuck to their script. We knew they held all the cards.

After Chris had his say, I started getting a bit worked up myself. I asked Archbishop Kurtz under what circumstance I might ever be allowed to return to Boy Scout leadership at Lourdes. He didn't answer my question directly, so I pressed on. I heatedly inquired that if I divorced my husband, would I then be eligible to return to leadership? Again, neither man offered me an answer. The irony of my suggestion, that I get a divorce from a marriage the Church didn't recognize in the first place, wasn't lost on anyone. The Church has long stood opposed to divorce, but would its refusal to recognize my same-sex marriage also prevent me from serving as a Scout leader?

The lack of real dialogue in the meeting was apparent. It felt like Chris and I, both Catholics, were being lectured to from a position of moral superiority. The emphasis from the Chancery was on restating doctrine and its obligation to enforce Church policies, and there could be no exceptions. We certainly weren't engaging in what Chris or I thought were meaningful discussion.

Our allotted time was over. We shook hands and parted ways respectfully. The Archdiocese had met its pastoral commitment to have a meeting. It could check that box.

As I walked out the front door and down the sidewalk to the parking lot, I was quite shaken. I could tell Chris was shaken, too, as we nervously debriefed ourselves. When we got to the end of the sidewalk, we started to go in different directions, but we couldn't leave it at that. We stopped and embraced for the longest time, long enough that I started to tremble and softly weep over the sheer emotion of what we had just experienced. I felt my sentiments pass slowly to Chris. Our emotions had been triggered as a result of that important but unfruitful encounter inside the Chancery. Chris and I had taken our naked faith and belief in fairness, equality, and social justice and argued our case for dignity and inclusion to Church leadership. We may not have won any war, but we stood strong in directly and personally delivering our arguments. We did our best to speak truth to power. Unfortunately, power did not seem to care much about what truth had to say.

30

LIFE AFTER SCOUTING

Resolved that the Archdiocese would never allow me to return to service as a registered leader with my Scout troop, I tried my best to move on by focusing on my career and helping our children finish up high school and plan for the future. They were entering junior and senior year, respectively, so Michael and I busied ourselves with coordinating college visits and applications and all the other support they needed for high school. One such activity was to coordinate a campus visit for our high school junior, Bryson, to one of my alma maters, Notre Dame, over fall break. As was often the case when we set up college visits, we included a classmate friend to help make the trip more enjoyable for all.

We made reservations through the Admissions Office at Notre Dame for a mid-October visit. Given the cordial and supportive letter and card exchanges with Reverend Jenkins, it seemed practical to attempt to set up a brief meeting with him during our visit. Of course, I knew how busy the president of a major university can be, so I seriously doubted he could find time to meet with us. Surprisingly he wrote back and agreed to set a meeting on the same day as our campus visit.

Exhausted from the last few years of fighting for equality in scouting and in marriage, I was trying to let many things go and settle back into as much a normal life as possible. My crusading was over, or at least it needed to go on the back burner for a while. It was a time to be silent and seek inner peace and tranquility. There is a time for everything, you know. Turn, turn, turn. But Michael decided it was time for him to press the issue a bit with a handwritten letter in early September to the Archbishop:

> Dear Archbishop Kurtz,
> I wanted to share a letter that was written 16 years ago when our child was baptized. It is a testament of our faith that these words ring so true today.
> Though your heart does not welcome LGBT Catholics we are assured that Jesus Christ does. If I was in your shoes, a shepherd for all God's flock, I would welcome good stewards of the Catholic faith.
> I pray for you daily and I ask that you do the same for me and my family. I am perplexed by the disconnect between you and the Holy Father. I pray that [the] Catholic Church revives itself in the United States. I believe that the Holy Father wants the Catholic Church to survive modern times.
> Regards,
> Michael De Leon

Archbishop Kurtz replied in kind with a handwritten note on September 15, 2015:

> Dear Mr. De Leon,
> May God bless you!
> I share with Pope Francis a recognition that we all are on the process of conversion toward greater holiness. All are invited to embrace Christ and His Church and all are welcome.
> You and your family are in my prayers.
> Sincerely yours in our Lord,
> Most Reverend Joseph E. Kurtz, D.D.
> Archbishop of Louisville

It was an affable enough response, one that seemed to signal he might be weary of the battle too. We gracefully and willingly entered a phase of peaceful coexistence. But I was still locked out of the Boy Scout troop, and there were frequent reminders of the unfairness of the Archdiocese toward its LGBTQ flock. Our local Archdiocesan weekly newspaper, *The Record*, continued to publish articles disparaging same-sex marriage, and other articles discouraging the support of adoptions by same-sex couples. It seemed like every time I read through *The Record*, there was something there to raise my blood pressure.

That same month, I was working as an Eagle Project coach with one of our Scouts from the troop at Lourdes. Long after I was ousted, my Scouts still kept coming to me for assistance; it was an honor to pitch in. Because I could not be a registered leader, I was greatly limited in what I could do to help the Scouts, but coaching Eagle Projects became my specialty. A few days after finishing up coaching that particular Eagle Project, my mentee sent a sweet note:

> Greg,
> You will never know how much it meant to me that you gave so much of your time last Saturday at E.P. to help me with my Eagle Project. I'm glad I completed it and without your support and re-minders I'm not quite sure I would have kept going. That day was totally exhausting—physically and emotionally. I am really proud of myself, thanks to you. Hopefully, you can give me some pointers for the Board of Review. Is that the next thing I do? I'll look in my workbook to see what to do next. Thanks,
> Seth

For those of you who have not been Scout leaders, this is precisely why we do it. Over my many years in scouting, I've received numerous notes and expressions of gratitude like that from my Scouts. They have been very thankful for the help and encouragement they needed to achieve rank advancement and other successes. That is why scouting is so important to me, and so that was why it was so atrocious that the Archdiocese prevented me from the kind of full-on leadership that would have benefited our Scouts so much more.

This was also the period when the Kim Davis scandal was erupting in eastern Kentucky. Davis was then the elected county clerk of Rowan County, who in August 2014 famously refused to issue same-sex marriage licenses in her county. Citing religious objections, Davis obstinately and frequently on camera refused to issue same-sex marriage licenses despite the SCOTUS ruling in *Obergefell*. After Davis defied a U.S. federal court order to issue same-sex marriage licenses, she ended up spending five days in jail for her violation of the law. Other activists tried to get Michael and me engaged in the protests and media campaign, but we were exhausted and tired of the fight. For the most part we decided it was best to let others handle that particular challenge. We had more than enough going on in our lives already just working and keeping up with our teenagers, not to mention my ninety-year-old parents.

The Kentucky plaintiffs, however, reengaged when the *Yale Law Review*, in its October Forum, published an article called "Perfect Plaintiffs." The author contended that the *Obergefell* plaintiffs were carefully cast because of their boring normalcy: "Thousands of videos, photographs, and articles tell their stories, emphasizing their ordinariness and approachability. In briefing and oral argument, attorneys described the couples' commitment to each other and to their many children. The strategy: Be normal."[26]

This set off a firestorm after the piece started circulating among the plaintiffs. We took turns tearing its premises to shreds. The very idea that the *Obergefell* plaintiffs were excruciatingly normal and painstakingly selected was ludicrous. First, we all had painful stories of mistreatment and discrimination that we shared with the media. Jim Obergefell being denied the opportunity to have his husband identified as married on the death certificate was just one of those examples of mistreatment. My heart breaks every time I hear Jim speak about the indignity of his treatment, and I'm pretty sure Jim's heart breaks too every time he has to talk about it. Many of the plaintiffs shared their painful stories with the media during this judicial process, and there was nothing normal about those circumstances.

If people did not grasp that concept, that we were a marginalized group, living in fear, being persecuted, being denied rights, paying unnecessary costs and taxes, and so on, well they just weren't listening to the whole story. The many court filings of the plaintiffs detailed the myriad ways in which our families had been discriminated against when the states did not recognize our families or allow us to marry. Those were the legal arguments that supported all of our cases. From our perspective, there was nothing normal or boring about people struggling against suppression and fighting for their legal rights and equal treatment under the

---

26. Cynthia Godsoe, "Perfect Plaintiffs," *The Yale Law Review* 125, no. 136 (2015), http://www.yalelawjournal.org/forum/perfect-plaintiffs.

law. The plaintiffs generally felt we had an obligation to stand up for ourselves and our families, for our rights, and for those like us who were not willing or able to make the stand that we did.

Second, it was also ridiculous that we'd been screened and cast for supposed "roles" as normal, ordinary Americans. There just weren't that many people willing to step up to challenge elected state officials, who had formidable resources and popular conservative support. There was so much risk that our attorneys really struggled to find ANY couples to press forward with a case. In no way did they have the luxury of picking the most "normal" ones with which to move forward.

There was much more analysis in the article, but we gradually accepted that it was an attempt at revisionist history. We knew painfully well our condition had not been normal. There had definitely not been a casting call. The *Obergefell* plaintiffs were not just like everyone else, but under the law we did want to be treated that way.

31

NOTRE DAME
OUR MOTHER

Fall Break arrived, and we made the five-hour drive from Louisville to South Bend to have an official campus visit at the University of Notre Dame. It had been a challenge to make it through the first two months of the school year after all the excitement that summer, so everyone was quite ready for fall break. Our son Bryson was a junior in high school, and we were taking opportunities to work in campus visits whenever we could.

Over the three bonus days afforded us during Fall Break, we made visits to two different campuses, but the trip to South Bend was the one I really looked forward to. Notre Dame's campus is, in my biased opinion, the most beautiful college campus anywhere in the country. When the fall colors are out, it can be extraordinarily striking.

After driving up the night before, we stayed at a hotel a few miles away from campus that was decorated throughout with a Notre Dame sports theme. The high schoolers I had with me were charmed with the hotel but even more impressed with the beautiful campus. Bryson had been on campus with our family many times over the years, but his friend with us was experiencing the beauty of Notre Dame for the very first time.

We had registered for an early morning information session at the Main Building. This is that iconic building you see during football games on television all the time with the golden dome and the enormous gilded statue of the Blessed Virgin on top. The information session was impressive. The speaker provided many statistics about how difficult it is to be accepted there, on the one hand, and how successful its graduates have been, on the other. Following the information session, we took a brief campus tour, hitting the highlights of the sprawling 1,261-acre campus.

Because Reverend Jenkins had scheduled a late morning appointment for us, we had to leave the walking tour group prematurely to scurry back to the Main Building. The President's Office is on the fourth floor of the massive Notre Dame administration building. The stairways that take you to the upper floors are beautiful, with curved wooden handrails spiraling up from floor to floor. As we climbed the stairs, it occurred to me I had no idea where the President's Office was. All I knew was it was on the top floor of the Main Building. I'd never been there before. I had met then President Theodore Hesburgh a few times when I was a student at Notre Dame in the early 1980s, but it was always out on campus somewhere. No doubt Father Hesburgh kept regular office hours, but I never had occasion to visit him there.

We were greeted kindly when we arrived at the receptionist desk and were escorted efficiently into Reverend Jenkins's office. It was a fine space befitting the president of a major university, with built-in wooden bookcases stuffed with books. There was a magnificent view of the heart of campus from his large fourth-floor windows.

Reverend Jenkins was a person of modest stature, not at all imposing or intimidating. He greeted us kindly and gently shook our hands. I couldn't help thinking his hands were a bit chilly, most likely because of the cold weather. He was a trim person with very well-defined features that didn't reflect his age. I sensed he was a person of incredible discipline when it came to matters of diet, exercise, and also intellectual pursuits.

Reverend Jenkins asked us to join him and sit in some easy chairs in a grouping that was away from his desk. He began the conversation as you might expect. He asked the high schoolers about their visit and what they thought of the campus. Bryson had been to campus dozens of times over the years for football games, basketball games, and summer visits in the Family Dorm. But the other student was experiencing Notre Dame for the very first time, gushing about the beauty of the campus and the holiness of the various sacred spaces we'd visited.

Eventually the topic shifted to LGBTQ inclusion on campus. Reverend Jenkins was again gracious about congratulating me on the historic Supreme Court decision that changed forever the way the country would define marriage. We didn't discuss Church doctrine on same-sex marriage because we both realized where that stood. Any substantial movement in that area was beyond our control. Instead we talked at length about the one thing we shared in common: our love for Notre Dame. We both wanted the university to continue its success, but I was concerned about expanding its diversity and inclusion efforts.

Reverend Jenkins had been a great advocate for strengthening and expanding many aspects of diversity and inclusion at Notre Dame, but one area that still seemed to lag was inclusion of LGBTQ staff, faculty, students, and alumni. Each group presented unique challenges for the university. I got the sense Reverend Jenkins truly wanted to do more, and faster. He told me he had many constituents to try to keep happy in running such a large and diverse organization. Consequently, change happens best when it's slow and measured.

Getting around to the most important reason for our visit with Reverend Jenkins, I asked again about the Notre Dame Alumni Association (NDAA). I hoped he could assist in getting it to officially recognize our Gay and Lesbian alumni group. Reverend Jenkins explained that the NDAA and the university were in the midst of a multiyear evaluation of its affinity programs and expected to have news on the subject soon. He then proudly offered reports on various other areas where the university had made some progress. In 2012, the university had founded its first-ever officially recognized club for LGBTQ students. There had been informal, unrecognized groups at ND for decades, including when I was on campus. The new student organization, called PRISM ND, had finally been launched under Jenkins's auspices, but many felt the restrictions placed on the group restrained its scope and activities.

Reverend Jenkins also shared that an LGBTQ Employee Resource Group for staff was in the making. He stated that his administration was responsible for launching same-sex partner health benefits at Notre Dame, much to the consternation of South Bend's conservative bishop. I did not verbalize this, but I suspected the employee group was launched to stop the bleeding of people who were leaving or wouldn't come to ND because of the lack of that institutional support. I also suspected the same-sex health benefits were adopted only because the *Obergefell* decision ruling was going to make it illegal not to offer them to married same-sex couples.

Nevertheless, I was thrilled that these changes were finally happening at ND. Thirty-five years after my graduation, the university was at least trying to play catch-up toward fuller LGBTQ equality and inclusion. It wasn't really important why it was happening; I only cared profoundly that it was.

When our meeting was drawing to a close, I asked Reverend Jenkins if we could take a few pictures. He gladly agreed and summoned his administrative assistant to facilitate the task. We snapped a few delightful pictures we could all use to remember the visit, said our goodbyes, and went our separate ways. As we left his office and walked down the stairs toward the exit, I had the real feeling that we had just met with one true disciple and authentic presence of Jesus on this earth. Humble, kind, cordial, intelligent, disciplined, pious, strong-willed. He had many admirable qualities. He'd actually blessed us with a block of time out of his busy schedule. I felt grateful to God for having sent such a wonderful representative to meet with us that on glorious, sunny, and cold October day in northern Indiana.

32

PRIDECATS

By this point I'd become deeply involved with the University of Louis-ville LGBT Center after having been a founder of the U of L LGBT Alumni Council. When the University of Kentucky finally began dupli-cating those initiatives in 2015, Michael and I contacted Lance Poston, the newly hired director of the UK Office of LGBTQ Resources, to offer our assistance. We encouraged Lance to develop a networking gala fund-raiser similar to the U of L's successful Feast on Equality event. We also initiated conversations about launching an LGBTQ Alumni Council at UK. Development work ensued to launch an LGBTQ alumni group or-ganized under the name "PrideCats," invoking the UK wildcat mascot.

In early December, UK held its inaugural LGBTQ Holiday Recep-tion. Michael and I were presented the First Annual University of Ken-tucky LGBTQ Alumni Award. When the award was presented, the organizers announced that henceforth it would be called the Bourke-DeLeon Distinguished LGBTQ Alumni Award. It would be granted annually at the UK holiday event.

It was an incredible honor for us, one that brought Michael and me back to our roots at UK where we met as students nearly thirty-five years earlier. By this point, UK seemed to recognize that Michael and I could be very helpful in launching various aspects of its diversity and inclusion efforts for UK's LGBTQ community. Within a week after the ceremony, we received an email from the executive assistant of Eli Capi-louto, president of UK, inviting Michael and me to a dinner at his pri-vate on-campus residence, Maxwell Place.

That evening of the dinner, we joined another dozen or so people as President Capilouto shared his enthusiasm over the marriage equality decision and his pride over the role UK grads had played in it. President Capilouto also showed great support and vision for a much more diverse and inclusive UK, one that had its LGBTQ student, staff, and alumni right in the center of the effort.

33

CATHOLIC PERSONS
OF THE YEAR

A few days later, just before Christmas, I received a cryptic email from Ross Murray at GLAAD. He'd received a media request from Dennis Coday at the *National Catholic Reporter*. Michael and I had received these types of heads-up so many times during the scouting and marriage equality efforts that I didn't give it much thought. Soon thereafter, Coday emailed me: "Each year we honor a Catholic (or in your case Catholics) who have made a significant contribution to the life of the U.S. Catholic Church that year. We selected you and Mr. DeLeon for 2015 because of your involvement with the Supreme Court ruling on same-sex marriage and for your longtime faithful witness as members of your Louisville parish."

At first I thought it was a joke. Somebody was scamming me. Next someone was probably going to ask me to wire money overseas to help them. But then I remembered the alert from GLAAD and realized it was authentic.

The news was quite unexpected, it was nearly impossible to process. Michael and I never practiced our faith with the intention of being recognized for it. That wouldn't be appropriate, it wouldn't be consistent with Christian values. We faithfully practiced our faith because that was how we were raised, because it was our own personal calling, and because it was something we truly enjoyed doing and sharing together. One should not practice faith with the intent of any recognition for it, because faith is its own reward, so getting this kind of recognition made me feel quite uncomfortable. But after some reflection I realized it could be beneficial for the advancement of LGBTQ inclusion in the Catholic Church, so I accepted it for what it was: more of God's mysterious work.

The email went on to note past honorees for the award:

2014—Pope Francis (Stephen Colbert was our runner up)
2013—Jennifer Haselberger, a Minnesota canon lawyer and whistle-blower on clergy sex abuse
2012—Chief Justice John Roberts
2011—St. Joseph Sr. Elizabeth Johnson, a theologian at Fordham University
2010 (our first)—Sr. Carol Keehan, the Daughter of Charity who is president and CEO of the Catholic Health Association

When I read the list of honorees, I didn't think we deserved to be in the company of such giants. All Michael and I had done was live relatively quiet and faithful lives of dedication to our faith and Church despite the lack of acceptance from the Church's hierarchy. We did our best to stand tall in our faith and stay devoted to our parish and dedicated to our Christian family, but that just didn't seem to stack up to the accomplishments of the other honorees. The most ironic thing about that list was that it also included Chief Justice Roberts, the man who cast his vote against marriage equality in *Obergefell* and delivered a scathing dissenting opinion.

34

CATHOLICS
FOR FAIRNESS

After the 2015 holidays, life got much calmer for the Bourke De Leon family. Michael and I began working with our hometown LGBTQ historian, David Williams, to pass some personal items to the Williams–Nichols Collection at the University of Louisville. Among other things it accepted were the neckties Michael and I wore on *Obergefell* decision day and a series of gay-themed sociology papers I'd written as an out gay student at U of L during the 1970s.

As the winter drew to a close, it was time for our annual Catholics for Fairness Rally and Pilgrimage in downtown Louisville. That year, Chris Hartman asked Michael and me to be keynote speakers, commemorating the receipt of the *National Catholic Reporter* Persons of the Year Award. A large and boisterous crowd showed up. People seemed determined to keep celebrating the marriage equality victory and everything it meant to them. Ad-libbing as I often do, I addressed a group of Sisters of Charity nuns in attendance to thank them for attending: "I learned everything I ever needed to know about social justice from the progressive Dominican nuns who taught me in elementary school at Saint Stephen Martyr."

To coordinate with our speaking at the Catholics for Fairness rally, Chris Hartman suggested I write an op-ed for the *Courier-Journal*, so I wrote and had published a commentary titled "Year of Mercy Should Extend to LGBT." Among other things, I argued:

There could be no better time than this Extraordinary Jubilee Year—only the third in Catholic history—for Louisville Archbishop Joseph E. Kurtz to join in a show of mercy and compassion for LGBT Kentuckians, who continue to be marginalized and face legal discrimination in our commonwealth.

Time and again, we have been made to feel shame and exclusion by the very church that teaches love, compassion, and mercy—our church. It is a travesty of God's true love for LGBT people and there is no better time for it to cease than this Jubilee Year of Mercy.[27]

The message seemed to get a favorable response. Numerous people stopped me at work the next Monday to congratulate me on its publication and offer their moral support. The Archdiocese of Louisville, on the other hand, did not respond in any way.

---

27. Greg Bourke, "Year of Mercy Should Extend to LGBT," *Courier-Journal*, March 10, 2016, https://www.courier-journal.com/story/opinion/2016/03/10/comment-year-mercy-should-extend-lgbt/81550596/.

35

THE FREEDOM
TO BURY

Back in the summer of 2015, my cousin Angela Bourke Schultz texted me. She worked in the sales department at Catholic Cemeteries for the Archdiocese of Louisville. Angie told me that some of the cemetery plots in the "coveted section 124" of Saint Michael's Cemetery were coming on the market soon. Saint Michael's had held a few open paths through the section for use by maintenance vehicles, but now it had decided it was time to sell those empty grave plots. Angie had sent out a group text to the whole local Bourke family because section 124 was where nearly all of the previous generations of Bourke relatives were buried or had already purchased plots. This provided a rare and unanticipated opportunity for us younger Bourkes to select a final resting place with the generations of Bourkes before us.

After some thought and discussion (who likes to talk about that?), Michael and I decided to purchase plots in the Bourke family section. We were approaching the age of sixty, so we wanted to relieve our children and other family from the potential burden of having to make rushed decisions during a time a grief.

After we purchased the plots in the summer of 2015, Michael and I scheduled a session with Angie to start planning our memorial. Angie met with us on a sunny October day at the Catholic Cemeteries offices in Calvary Cemetery and began the process of discussing what our memorial might look like. After looking through some sample books in the sales office, she suggested we drive through Calvary and Saint Michael's cemeteries, which are both owned by the Archdiocese, to view some real-life monuments.

After we got out of the busy Archdiocesan cemetery office and into her car, Angie confidentially informed us that since the *Obergefell* decision, the Archdiocese of Louisville had initiated a new memorial approval policy. The Archdiocese would need to review and approve memorials for any same-sex couple wishing to be buried in a Louisville Catholic Cemetery. This new policy required an approval that did not apply to opposite-sex couples. No one had been denied any designs (yet), so she didn't want us to get too concerned. But how could we not get concerned since it was enacted seemingly in response to the marriage equality ruling with the intent of purposefully discriminating against same-sex couples?

Angie drove us through the cemeteries. We visited memorials for some of our relatives, and she pointed out many other installed memorials for our consideration. Michael and I consider ourselves modest people and have no desire in death to present any image not conformed to in life. We wanted a small headstone consistent in size and presentation to those in the section where we'd be buried.

One important distinction was that nearly all the married couples in section 124 had interlocking rings on their memorials, so we decided this was a design element we wanted to include. Other than that, we developed a very basic design with our names, birth dates, and a space for our dates of death to be engraved later. Two other graphic elements were included: a cross to represent our Christian faith, and a small, whimsical graphic of the U.S. Supreme Court Building.

As we drove around Saint Michael's Cemetery, we saw a wide range of such graphics. One depicted the twin spires at Churchill Downs and another a man fly-fishing. One was shaped and engraved like a car radiator. After making all the relevant decisions about stone types and finish and piecing together a final design, we left the rest to Angie. We exchanged numerous emails and considered various proposals and prices. By mid-October we decided on a final design, but Angie told us it had to go through the Archdiocesan approval process before we could move forward. The waiting began.

Over the next several months, I kept checking back with Angie to ask about the approval status and progress. As a first cousin and dear friend, I didn't want to pressure her too much, but I could sense in our exchanges there was information she was holding back. As the waiting period lengthened through Halloween, Thanksgiving, Christmas, and New Year, we still couldn't get an approval or any definitive feedback on our proposed monument. The calendar rolled over to 2016. Through the harshness of winter, the wait continued with still no approval. Finally, on March 30, 2016, we received a letter from Javier Fajardo, the executive director of Catholic Cemeteries.

His letter started by thanking us for our patience as they considered our proposed monument for the gravesite we purchased at Saint Michael's Cemetery. It started with good news to "reaffirm your decision to have Saint Michael Cemetery serve as your burial site at some time in the future." Those words at least reassured us we would in fact be able to be buried there—and together. But then the bad news:

> Having reviewed your proposed gravestone inscription please note that we can approve your shared stone with both your names and dates of birth and of course the religious symbol of the cross. However we cannot approve the depiction of the Supreme Court building and the use of wedding rings.
>
> Inscriptions on grave markers are permitted so long as they do not conflict with any teachings of the Church. Your proposed markings are not in keeping with this requirement. Determination as to the appropriateness of any inscription or symbol is the judgement of the Executive Director of Catholic Cemeteries in consultation with proper Church authority.

There was some good news. We would be allowed to have a shared stone. That much would be permitted. But it was particularly disappointing they weren't going to allow the interlocking rings. Michael and I had intentionally passed on including a "married date" on the memorial despite the fact those are extremely common for married couples buried in Saint Michael's Cemetery. We decided not to push things that far to avoid potential controversy. Given what we had seen on other headstones in that cemetery (e.g., graphic images of the Louisville cardinal and Kentucky wildcat mascots), it did not appear there was any consideration given to what people wanted displayed graphically on their memorials. Having seen on a memorial in Saint Michael's an image of Churchill Downs's twin spires, how exactly does an image of the Supreme Court Building conflict with any teaching of the Church? When we got the news, it felt very much like we were being targeted once again because of our participation in the marriage equality decision. It felt like retaliation. It felt like discrimination. It hurt.

We knew Saint Michael's was a private Catholic cemetery, so we realized we had no legal leg to stand on if we tried to challenge the decision. The City of Louisville has a broad LGBTQ Fairness Ordinance that protects queer people from discrimination in areas of employment, housing, and public accommodations. But when the ordinance was passed in 1999, an exemption for religious organizations had to be included. This right to discriminate by religious organizations in Louisville had been used quite frequently against LGBTQ people. Our altered stone was just one more case of a faith-based organization intentionally using that option on an already marginalized group of people.

Without a viable option for a legal challenge, Michael and I brought our concerns to Chris Hartman at the Fairness Campaign so that he could at least be aware of the Archdiocese's latest offense. Chris was as outraged as we were, and he was determined to do something to raise awareness about this latest case of Church-sponsored discrimination against LGBTQ people. He proposed some alternatives. He suggested a protest at one of the public appearances or masses the Archbishop would be making over the coming weeks. That would be tricky because there weren't many options at good times or on days where Chris could mobilize his volunteer base to participate. Instead, he concluded a protest and press conference at Saint Michael's Cemetery would be most effective for getting the word out.

Michael and I went on about our busy lives of work and parenting, but Chris, who had many years of experience at organizing such events, mobilized his resources. An email blast went out to Fairness Campaign supporters: "We are going to hold a press conference outside St. Michael's Cemetery next Wednesday, May 18, at 10:00 a.m. to draw attention to the Archdiocese of Louisville's continual snubs of this deeply committed Catholic family." He included a copy of our design and the rejection letter from Catholic Cemeteries and encouraged people to show up in support. Next, he got the word out to the local media. Chris had very good and deep relationships with the media. They had covered and supported his efforts with great dedication and sympathy over the years. There was considerable speculation among the local media about what the press conference might involve, but Chris made us agree to keep it quiet and not take media requests for days in advance in order to build interest.

On the day of the press conference, Michael and I arrived early. There were already several television and print reporters on hand. There was a featured speaker, Jim Wayne, a Kentucky state representative and cofounder of the Catholics for Fairness movement. The supportive protesters rolled in, along with more media, and at 10 a.m. the press conference began.

Chris kicked things off by explaining the purpose of the gathering. After laying the groundwork, he turned the event over to Michael and me to tell in detail the full story of our memorial's denial. We showed pictures of many of the other memorials in Saint Michael's, including the ones with the strange and bizarre images. It made a compelling presentation. Why us?, we wanted to know. Why, just now, was this newly crafted policy being enforced?

Jim Wayne, a masterful orator and widely respected state politician, took over to lay out his case against the Church for its shameful discrimination against a class of people it had already profoundly marginalized. After a question-and-answer session, we took a walk across the street and into the cemetery with cameras following us. I identified the many memorials in section 124 for my deceased family members. It was a very emotional walk, pointing out relatives and thinking about how many of them had experienced discrimination as Irish immigrants and Catholics at various stages in their lives in Kentucky. Of course, we didn't think the press conference would actually convince the Archdiocese to change its decision on our memorial, but it seemed important to at least raise awareness about the discrimination we were forced to accept at the hands of our own Church.

36

SUMMER BREAK

Shortly after the freedom to bury episode played out, Isaiah graduated from Catholic high school in May, and we found relief from the school year grind. Early June 2016 brought yet another trip to South Bend so I could participate on a panel at Reunion Weekend to again raise awareness about the exclusion of the GALA group from official affinity group recognition at the University of Notre Dame. That was my third year on the panel. Each year it took increasing measures of patience and grace to have to listen to people in the audience rail about the university and how it was unfair and cruel not to formally admit the LGBTQ alumni group. They would also challenge and criticize GALA for not doing more to force the issues with the university administration and the Notre Dame Alumni Association. Some thought more drastic and confrontational approaches, even lawsuits, should be pursued to try to force progress and recognition. People were often angry and frustrated over what appeared to be the lack of any progress whatsoever. Each year I endured this interrogation, it wore me down a bit more, but it also served as inspiration to keep working to eliminate this barrier and pursue LGBTQ inclusion in the Notre Dame Alumni Association.

A few days later, Lance Poston, director of the Office of LGBTQ Resources at UK, contacted Michael and me with an invitation to join a group of UK grads for dinner at Table 310, a restaurant in downtown Lexington. His goal was to try to organize and launch an LGBTQ alumni council, something we'd been encouraging UK to do. Lance carefully selected about a dozen Kentucky alumni and asked them to consider his proposal about forming such a group at UK. By the end of the evening, everyone agreed to participate and serve on an inaugural advisory board. We selected "PrideCats" for our name. The group committed to work on a charter. Tuesday Meadows would be its leader. This meant I was now a member at-large, board member, or officer on three separate LGBTQ university alumni groups, and I'd been a founding member for two of them. Needless to say, I was feeling stretched a little thin, but when duty calls it's best just to suck it up and roll with it.

On June 12, 2016, Michael and I had the joyous occasion to attend the baptism of a newborn that had been adopted by a gay couple we knew. We knew they were interested in starting a family, so Michael had a significant role in lining up the adoption for them. When Michael learned that our neighbor, an adoption attorney, was working with an expectant mother looking for a good family to adopt her child, he got to work playing matchmaker, and it worked out. The fact that our friends were a devout Catholic couple and having their baby adopted at a local Catholic church made the event all the sweeter. On the way to the baptism, we casually checked our phones and saw breaking news about another mass shooting, this one at a nightclub in Orlando in the wee hours of that morning. We didn't know it yet, but that shooting at Pulse nightclub would end up being the worst massacre of LGBTQ people in U.S. history.

As the day wore on, we tried to celebrate a baptism and reception, but the horrifying details of the massacre kept coming out and the mood got grimmer. By late afternoon we learned that in the evening there would be a rally and march at a pedestrian bridge over the Ohio River in downtown Louisville to mourn the victims and show support for the LGBTQ community. Michael and I decided to attend, but we thought only a few dozen people would show up. We were shocked when a massive crowd estimated at 5,000, including the mayor and many other elected officials, showed up to walk the bridge and pay tribute to the fallen. When we stopped the march halfway across the bridge and sang "We Shall Overcome," it was one of the most powerful experiences of my life. There wasn't a dry eye on the bridge.

The next day at work I expected there would be endless chatter about the shooting as there had been for every other mass shooting over the years. Working in an open office for many years, I knew that people loved to talk about current events, especially controversial news happenings like mass shootings. This time it was different, though. This time not a person said a word. I couldn't believe what I was not hearing. Day after day that week I waited for someone to bring up the topic or at least for someone to ask how I was doing, but it never happened.

Finally, several days into the silence I sent a post to our internal company social media platform called Buzz. I was stunned that people were not talking. They didn't seem to care at all about forty-nine lives that had been snuffed out. Didn't it bother them that such a heinous hate crime could be perpetrated on so many innocent victims? After I posted my rant, one co-worker ally who saw it approached me and we had a private conversation in a meeting room. He had also noticed the peculiar silence on the subject and offered his support. In the next day or two the company finally responded. Associates who needed counseling over the trauma could do so through the employee assistance program. But it was too little too late. Those scars from the sounds of silence still live with me.

A few weeks later, our family had the opportunity to go to Washington, DC, to participate in the one-year anniversary celebrations for the *Obergefell* marriage equality decision. The Human Rights Campaign held a press conference and a photo shoot at the Supreme Court Building, and there was a benefit at its headquarters with several of the *Obergefell* plaintiffs in attendance. There was unfortunately a bit of a somber mood. Many were still grieving the Pulse nightclub massacre.

After we wrapped up in DC, our family did exactly what it had done the previous year: we took the train to New York to march again as a family with the Scouts for Equality honor guard. This time I had my uniform, and like a good Scout was thoroughly prepared. For the New York Pride March in 2016 those not presenting the ceremonial flags carried forty-nine smaller flags commemorating the names of the fallen at Pulse nightclub.

After returning to Louisville, we learned on social media that a Catholic church in Lexington was planning an interfaith memorial service for the Pulse victims. Not only was it a Catholic church, but it was the specific Catholic church where Michael and I used to attend Mass each Sunday right after we met in the early 1980s: Saint Paul the Apostle in downtown Lexington. Since the Catholic community in Louisville was not acknowledging or offering support for grieving LGBTQ people, Michael and I decided we'd drive over to Lexington.

Saint Paul's worship director, JR Zerkowski, had carefully and compassionately organized the interfaith service, and we were blessed that night to meet him for the first time. The event wasn't intended to be anything else, but it essentially served as the launch for an LGBTQ ministry at Saint Paul: the first of its kind at a Catholic parish in our part of the country. That evening at the memorial, Michael and I also had the opportunity to meet Lexington bishop John Stowe, who endorsed and defended the need for the LGBTQ ministry at Saint Paul. Both JR and Bishop Stowe would eventually become outspoken leaders for LGBTQ Catholics. We are grateful that our paths have continued to cross often over the years.

37

ADOPTION DAY— THE SEQUEL

One of the very first things we did after the *Obergefell* decision was to focus on the goal of completing the second-parent adoption of our two children. This had been the primary motivation for filing our marriage equality case in the first place. We wanted to work with the initial attorneys from the *Bourke v. Beshear* case, Shannon Fauver and Dawn Elliott, but neither had experience with family law adoptions. As a result, we had to be patient as they worked through the legal steps.

Michael and I had to schedule a family meeting with a state social worker who would fill out some forms and interview our family about the desired adoption. By that time our children were sixteen and seventeen, but they didn't fully comprehend the benefits of this legal move at first. We explained to them it was important for long-term considerations and potential inheritance rights. After plodding through that meeting with the social worker, we waited and waited. After numerous follow-ups, we finally got a date in Family Court for July 29, 2016, more than a year after *Obergefell* was decided.

The Family Court judge was thrilled to be able to oversee our proceedings. She even gladly took pictures with our family in the courtroom along with our attorneys. She said it was a pleasure to have a court proceeding for such a happy occasion because most of what she dealt with in Family Court was not so pleasant. It was a day of triumph for our family. After co-parenting for more than sixteen years, both of us were finally recognized as *equal parents under the law*. It shouldn't have been that difficult, but that's how things worth waiting for in life often work.

Of course, a parent's work is never done. After the adoption was final, we still had to contend with the Social Security Administration. Then we had to go through the tedious process of getting birth certificates modified and changing our children's status to reflect that they had, indeed, two parents. To finish the process and wrap up the last of our legal loose ends, Michael and I had to meet with our regular attorney, fellow Lourdes parishioner Allan Dunaway. He helped us craft wills and some other documents to show we were in fact finally legally married. What a long haul it had been to get to that point, but it was satisfying to finally have these pesky details behind us.

That summer I made it a priority to schedule several lunches with my former fellow Scout leader, Don Overton. Don had been diagnosed with cancer and was undergoing radiation therapy, so I knew our time together might be limited. He had had a grandson in the Lourdes Boy Scout troop for many years, and Don was my longtime mentor as a Scout leader. Mister Overton, as everyone called him, and I took the troop to full weeks at summer camp for six years in a row. Our very first year together at camp, we were at a volunteer leader appreciation dinner when out of the blue my new friend Don saw my wedding ring and asked me about my wife. Lowering my voice a bit so the other scouters wouldn't hear, I told him I didn't have a wife, I had a husband. Without skipping a beat, Don said simply, "Okay then."

Mister Overton wasn't the kind of person you would expect to be LGBTQ-supportive. He was a somewhat conservative, Episcopal priest from Oklahoma and a retired military chaplain. But Don had such a love for scouting and knew we shared that passion, so we were bound together for many years in our service to that cause. The prospect of Don passing only brought us closer together. When he was finally gone, it was a blow to both our troop and to me personally. His family offered me the great honor of serving as a pallbearer at his funeral. Years later I still keep his obituary taped on my office wall to remind me of his abundant love and call to service for all of God's people.

38

PILGRIMAGE
OF MERCY

In late summer of 2016, Jack Bergen, chair of the Gay and Lesbian Alumni of Notre Dame and Saint Mary's (GALA ND/SMC) told me the alumni group was going to have a benefit for its LGBTQ scholarship in a few months. The event would take place at the NYC Fifth Avenue penthouse residence of Phil Donahue, a Notre Dame alumnus and long-time supporter of gay rights, and his wife, the actress Marlo Thomas. At first he described it as just another invite to a fundraiser. But then he told me he'd be honored if I'd serve as the keynote speaker:

> The work you and your husband have done, both in the scouts and with marriage equality, has been a tremendous driving force for change, and we would love to have you share with the guests (mostly ND grads) your experience and impact in creating change. In addition, we are thinking of having an activity to promote greater inclusion by Notre Dame, and the Catholic church in general, and had thought of using the "Year of Mercy" as the vehicle to use for this (similar to the walk you recently did as publicized in the *Courier-Journal*).

It was one thing to stand up at a cocktail party and say a few words to a friendly crowd and then ask them for money to support the LGBTQ scholarships at Notre Dame and Saint Mary's. It was another thing entirely to create an event in New York City that duplicated what it had taken years to develop in Louisville. Feeling bolstered by the success of the *Obergefell* marriage equality case, and motivated to do something more in the wake of the freedom to bury rejection, I told Jack Bergen to sign me up for both, and I would figure the rest of it out later.

Jack added me to the planning committee with other Notre Dame and Saint Mary's alums and held regular conference calls to plan the details. To duplicate the Louisville event would require a rally location, a pilgrimage march route, and a welcoming Catholic church where marchers could attend Mass together as a group. The local ND and SMC alums from New York offered a half dozen churches that were friendly or sympathetic to LGBTQ inclusion. After long debate, we decided the pilgrimage should end at Saint Paul the Apostle, which had a very active LGBT ministry called Out at Saint Paul. It was adjacent to Central Park, which would enable the use of park pathways for the pilgrimage. The rally could also be held in the park along the way.

Phil Donahue was enthusiastic at the prospect of the pilgrimage and very much wanted to participate. Since Pope Francis had declared 2016 to be an official "Extraordinary Jubilee Year of Mercy," the planning committee agreed that the pilgrimage should also carry that name. A good starting point, it determined, was just outside Phil's building, which overlooked Central Park on the east side. The event plan called for participants to meet there and have a press conference, then march through the park and rally at the edge near Columbus Circle before going into Mass at Saint Paul.

It took many weeks of preparation to put the details together so it all made sense, flowed, and did not violate any city ordinances. But the event still needed one more thing: someone to lead the rally. At that point I called upon the master of rally enthusiasm, Chris Hartman, to join us in New York and lead participants through all phases of the pilgrimage. It was a tremendous relief when he agreed, primarily because that particular burden wouldn't fall on me! At any rate, nobody runs a rally better than Chris.

We next needed to work on recruiting people to participate. The first invites were the dozens of Notre Dame and Saint Mary's alums planning to attend the GALA ND/SMC benefit at the Donahue penthouse later that same day. I also engaged my personal network to help promote the pilgrimage. Working with past collaborators from GLAAD, ACLU,

Human Rights Campaign, Freedom to Marry, New Ways Ministries, Dignity, Fortunate Families, Out at Saint Paul, and many others, we got the word out and invited affiliates to come and support the effort. In the process of building awareness, I told the LGBTQ-supportive bishop in Lexington about it and requested his prayers. His response on September 7, 2016, warmed my heart and gave me great hope:

> Dear Greg,
> I wish both of you every success. I hope that the Mercy Pilgrimage is meaningful for all who participate. You can count on my prayers.
> Bishop John Stowe, OFM Conv.
> Diocese of Lexington

One of the ND alums on the pilgrimage planning committee was acquainted with Matthew Putorti, who was active in the Out at Saint Paul. Matt contacted the pastor, Father Gil, on our behalf and convinced him to host the event and welcome pilgrimage participants who wanted to attend Mass.

On Sunday, October 2, Michael and I walked from our midtown Manhattan hotel to Central Park on the Fifth Avenue side just outside the front door of Phil Donahue's building. Soon Chris Hartman showed up. After exchanging greetings, we shared our fears about throwing a party and having no one come. But soon enough they did start showing up. Although the turnout was lighter than desired, we ended up with a very respectable assembly of pilgrims. When Phil Donahue came down and joined us in the park, the media became very attentive and the cameras started rolling. Several of the organizers spoke with the press. Then the pilgrimage kicked off along the outskirts of Central Park.

Michael and I walked with Andy Humm, a well-known LGBTQ reporter for *Gay USA*. We ended up talking with him for much of the walk. Andy had many questions about how Michael and I reconciled our faith with the often unsupportive and discriminatory policies of the Church toward LGBTQ people. Not only have LGBTQ people been denied legal marriage equality, but they also have been denied by the Church what is referred to as "sacramental equality" in being prohibited from participating in the sacrament of marriage with their same-sex partner. In addition, many gay and lesbian employees of the Church have had to live closeted lives in fear of being exposed and face retaliation. Church leaders have been painfully unforgiving about firing gay and lesbian employees over just the suspicion of an alternative sexual orientation or being involved in a same-sex marriage.

This was a conversation Michael and I had been having with various people for more than thirty years, so the answers came easy. Usually the person listening to the answers responds with a look of skepticism. But Andy understood the message that has become our personal motto: "If we leave, they win." For years that sentiment has motivated us to stay and fight for our faith and our rightful place in God's Church. The easy solution would have been to simply leave and surrender that ground, but that is not the path we chose. God rarely calls one to take the easy path.

The pilgrimage stopped at Columbus Circle, and Chris, with his trusty travel microphone and speaker, launched the rally with great flair and enthusiasm. There were many speakers, but each kept their comments brief. That was the format we used at the Louisville Catholics for Fairness rallies. The pilgrims were blessed to hear inspiring words of faith and encouragement from Francis DeBernardo, executive director of New Ways Ministry; Holly Cargill-Cramer from Fortunate Families; me; and Phil Donahue. Perhaps the most compelling speaker of the day was Warren Hall, a priest who'd been fired by the Catholic Seton Hall University in South Orange, New Jersey, for his support of LGBTQ rights. Warren's expulsion from his job and essentially his ministry was timely and in the news. His plea for a more compassionate and inclusive Church was one that resounded with us all.

After the rally, most of the pilgrims walked the few blocks from Columbus Circle to Saint Paul the Apostle Church and peacefully attended Mass together with the regular parishioners. After Mass, Michael and I spoke with Father Gil and thanked him for his hospitality. He told us he'd gotten some heat that week from people outside Saint Paul who did not want him to welcome our group. It had also been suggested he should not offer Holy Communion to us. We all found the news rather perplexing because withholding Communion from any Catholic faithfully and reverently seeking it certainly does not seem what Jesus would have done.

After Mass, we moved on to the GALA ND/SMC scholarship benefit at Phil and Marlo's penthouse. It was a great relief to have the pilgrimage behind us, but I felt exhausted. Still, I had to deliver some kind of coherent remarks to the attendees. Working with only a few handwritten talking points, I really don't remember much of what I said except for one thing.

The program opened with wonderful comments by both Phil and Marlo. When it was my turn, I saw an opportunity to ad-lib and veer from my notes a bit. I noted that there was a 1970s theme going on that night. First, we heard from Phil from *The Phil Donahue Show* and then Marlo from the popular television sitcom *That Girl*. In my native Kentucky drawl, I commented that apparently I was there to represent *The Beverly Hillbillies*. It proved to be an effective icebreaker, but more than anything it helped put me at ease. It was a night to celebrate a successful peaceful rally and pilgrimage, to celebrate ND/SMC LGBTQ scholarship recipients, who were also on hand, and a night to celebrate once again the progress achieved with marriage equality.

39

RECONCILIATION

By late 2016, Michael's parents had passed years before, and my elderly parents, both in their nineties, had gone into sharp physical and mental decline. My three brothers and I had been providing caregiver services to them over several years so they could remain in their home, as they desired. We finally started using home healthcare with my parents during the workweek. On weekends my brothers and I attended to their pills, meals, housework, and other things. For a few years Michael and I had started taking them to Mass with us on Saturday evenings at Lourdes, and then they would come over to our house for dinner. It was a bit of a nuisance because it required driving across town to pick them up, then transporting them (and the walker and wheelchair) back to their home after dinner. After many years of being 9:30 a.m. Sunday worshipers at Lourdes, Michael and I became regulars at Saturday evening services. In doing so we came to know and love an entirely different group of fellow parishioners.

We were never sit-up-front churchgoers, but when Mom and Dad started going to church with us, we'd sit in the front pew so they wouldn't have to walk down the aisle to the altar to receive Holy Communion. Over those years, my parents became de facto parishioners at Lourdes because everyone grew accustomed to seeing us there with them in the first pew. On Saturday morning each week I'd check in with Mom and Dad and ask if they wanted to go to Mass and dinner that evening. As their health further declined and the weeks and months passed, often they decided to skip church, so I would just take them dinner and Michael and I would go to Mass without them.

It's difficult to watch those you love decline and face their inevitable future, but that caused me to reflect on where I was in life and what unfinished business I might have left if suddenly taken from this existence. My thoughts turned to the resentment I harbored toward those who had ousted me as Scout leader and kept me from returning in that capacity. Specifically I was still upset toward those people at the Archdiocese of Louisville who had mobilized to marginalize my family from full inclusive participation in our Church. Even after we had been fighting for and winning legal recognition as a married couple and family, the Church still did not recognize us as married or a family, and it had taken action to make sure I personally could not return to a leadership role in the Scout unit at Lourdes.

As a Christian I knew that resentment was not healthy or sustainable. Jesus called each of us to live without passing judgment on others and to strive to both give and receive forgiveness and reconciliation. My prayer and reflection allowed me to resolve the bitterness I'd been experiencing with the Archdiocese and occasionally with Archbishop Kurtz. Over the following months I sent a few of cards and letters to our archbishop. I took the most conciliatory tone I could, considering our history of friction. To my pleasant surprise, Archbishop Kurtz responded in like tenor.

Later that year, a longtime member of our parish, Joanne Golden, the wife of Deacon Tim Golden, passed away and the funeral was scheduled at Lourdes. Michael and I knew the Goldens and wanted to pay our respects by attending the funeral. By this point Michael was singing regularly in the Resurrection Choir that performed at Lourdes funerals. On that day, November 3, 2016, Michael had already entered the church, so we arrived separately for the funeral. Below is a Facebook post I made later. My social media followers were a bit astonished.

This morning I attended the funeral Mass of a fellow parishioner at Lourdes. As I entered the gathering space, I noticed there was a large group of deacons and priests congregating that included Archbishop Kurtz. We saw each other across the space, and Archbishop walked over and extended his hand and said, "Greg, thank you for your card." I replied, "Thank you for your leadership, Archbishop." As we shook hands and went on about our respective business.

Last week I sent Archbishop a card letting him know that I was praying for him often, and that I appreciated his service to our Church.

As we prayed the Lord's Prayer during Mass, it struck me that Archbishop and I have so much more in common than our some-times-public differences. Archbishop Kurtz has an incredibly diffi-cult job, and I would encourage anyone so inclined to join me in praying for and supporting him.

This was not only a real turning point for my relationship with the archbishop and the Archdiocese but also a great personal growth mo-ment for me. What good does it do to hold on to resentment? Jesus taught us to forgive. He died so we could be free from sin and live our lives in his love and free from such baggage. From that day on I have been at peace. My sometimes contentious relationship with the archbishop and the Archdiocese is behind me. What good had squabbling done us? None. I decided to call a truce at least from my side and instead try prayer and reconciliation. Realizing we have so much more in common in our faith and the great traditions of our Church, we had no choice but to move forward together. The Church was not going anywhere. Neither were Michael and I.

My father passed away early the next year after a brief illness. The people at Lourdes were incredibly gracious, offering prayers for Dad and our whole family. Many Lourdes parishioners attended his visitation and funeral, even though Dad was buried out of his own parish, Saint Louis Bertrand. Losing my father at age ninety-two was still a challenge for me. I suppose no one is ever ready to give up that type of lifelong connection. My father and I shared a very good relationship. I know he was proud of who I was and what I'd accomplished in life. He was a loving force that provided great stability and guidance to me over the course of my life. Moving forward without him was going to be difficult.

Almost immediately after his passing, we realized that my mother needed to have around-the-clock care. After a thorough evaluation by a social worker from a local Catholic retirement community, my family agreed she should move into the memory care unit at Nazareth Home.

After she moved into the home, I convinced her a few times to come with us to Mass at Lourdes and over to our house for dinner, but nothing was the same for any of us after Dad passed. Eventually Mom just settled in at Nazareth Home, and I did my best to visit her every chance I got, which was quite often.

40

THE ANCIENT ORDER
OF HIBERNIANS

God presented me with another interesting calling about that time to officially become a member of the Ancient Order of Hibernians (AOH).

For those who are not familiar with it, AOH is a fraternal organization for people of Irish descent who are also active and practicing Catholics. It's been described as the Irish Knights of Columbus, an image that fits it well. It's devoted to both the Church and our Irish heritage. Because Hibernian membership requires close affiliation with the Catholic Church, many of its members tend to be conservative religiously and politically.

My brother Tim and his wife had been Hibernian members for years, as had an uncle, a nephew, and a cousin. All Bourkes. Various Hibernians had been trying to convince me to join for a while. Being openly gay, I always hesitated to join over concerns I wouldn't fit in or wouldn't be welcomed. Michael and I did attend numerous Hibernian events as guests before I joined. We particularly enjoyed the Irish New Year celebration, which was held at 7 p.m. local time when it was midnight in Dublin. As it turned out, the Hibernians had no concern at all with our being a same-sex couple and treated us with kindness and hospitality.

AOH meetings discuss a lot of things with the understanding their members won't disclose what goes on, so I can't share many details. I will say that I was nervous about joining. This required my making an appeal for acceptance to the AOH brothers, followed by a member vote to allow admission. Would the assembly of AOH brothers rebuff my attempt to join because I was so openly and publicly gay and had experienced past friction with the Archdiocese? Ultimately those fears proved unwarranted. Reflecting on that time now, I find it amusing I was so worried. Since then I've been on the other side, evaluating new candidates and reflecting how needlessly worried I'd been.

The Louisville division of AOH hasn't been the only part of the organization that's welcomed me with open arms. In the summer of 2018, the AOH National Convention was held in Louisville. For the entire four days of events, Michael and I were greeted by AOH brothers and sisters from all over the country. We presented ourselves as a married couple just like many other opposite-sex couples attending. Remarkably, or maybe not, no one seemed to care one bit that a same-sex married couple had been assimilated into this venerable Irish Catholic institution.

In the AOH, I've found a large new family of Irish Catholic brothers and sisters. They have welcomed Michael and me as a married couple unconditionally in ways that have been truly surprising. As far as I know, there are not any other openly gay members of the AOH anywhere in the United States, so we are grateful for the prospect of opening these doors for future members.

41

SCOUTING ON
THE FRINGE

Because it's one role that doesn't require me to be a registered leader, my work as an Eagle Project coach for several of my former Scouts has continued. In late March 2018, I received a very unexpected and pleasant surprise. It arrived in the mail, a card from a former Scout of mine whose family left Kentucky for Louisiana a few years ago for a new job opportunity. He was one of my favorites, a plucky little guy with boundless energy and enthusiasm who became our youngest senior patrol leader ever.

I was surprised that this Scout, now practically a young adult, had recently completed his Eagle rank at a Boy Scout troop in Louisiana. After he left, I was able to keep up with him and his family through the years and was able to help him a bit with encouragement, recommendations, and records to support different achievements from his time in our troop. When I found out he was about to have his Eagle Court of Honor, I went to our local Scout shop, as I typically do for my Scouts, bought him an Eagle gift, packaged it up with a commemorative card, and shipped it off.

In return he sent me a beautiful thank-you card, which is nothing extraordinary, but what touched me deeply was what else was inside. He'd sent me his Eagle Mentor pin. If and when Scouts finally achieve Eagle rank, they get to award this pin to the person of their choice who most influenced them on the road to this achievement, as my son Isaiah had done for me. Often these pins go to parents or Scoutmasters, but I've received a few of them from Scouts over the years. In the thank-you card he wrote, "I cannot express my gratitude towards the contributions you have made to my life enough. You are the reason I love scouting and made it all the way Eagle."

None of the previous Eagle Mentor pins I received ever had that effect on me. Each time I read this card, I tear up. I still have not been able to force myself to remove the pin from the card. The presentation is so meaningful and precious to me that I don't want to disturb it in any way.

Anybody who's spent time as a Scout leader knows it's an all-consuming and very often thankless job. Nobody who does it expects to receive any payback or recognition whatsoever. So when it happens, it can be overpowering. I suppose no one knows what kind of influence we are having on other people's lives when we're just out there living our own. We're all given at least a few opportunities to make a difference in someone else's life. For those who choose to serve others instead of serving themselves, the rewards can be astounding.

42

BOURKE DeLEON ENDOWED LGBT CATHOLIC SCHOLARSHIP

For years, Michael and I have been members of LGBTQ alumni groups at UK, U of L, and Notre Dame that awarded scholarships to LGBTQ students. Having done our part to contribute to fundraisers for each of those schools over the years, we experienced a calling to find a way to do more. We did some preliminary research into the endowment requirements with each of my alma maters to figure out which institution looked like the best home for a substantial financial gift.

As I was driving to work one morning and thinking about a potential scholarship, a thought popped into my mind. This is what you need to do, Greg: set up an endowed scholarship for LGBTQ Catholic students. This was certainly the will of God once again being revealed to me in a time and place that was most unexpected. God was providing direction on how to best proceed with this project.

Michael and I settled on U of L primarily because it is our hometown university and one with which we already had deep ties. Over several months we had meetings and exchanged emails and notes with Denise Bohn, an advancement professional at U of L, who helped us work through the details.

Each year the U of L Pride Alumni Council hosts an Alternative Thanksgiving on campus early in that holiday week. LGBTQ students who can't go home or aren't welcome at home are invited to a potluck on campus. It draws hundreds of students, faculty, staff, and alumni. In 2018 at this event, Michael and I were able to announce the new Bourke De-Leon Endowed LGBT Catholic Scholarship for students at U of L. Our announcement made an already feel-good event feel a lot better. Those present were thankful for the many blessings of our shared community that evening.

U of L has experienced more than its share of scandal over the last few years, including alleged mismanaged funds in the University of Louisville Foundation. There have also been integrity issues at different levels in staff, student athletics, and the administration. U of L took painful but necessary steps to steady the ship. With the hiring in 2018 of its new president, Neeli Bendapudi, it had made the right moves to reinstill confidence.

The university had been struggling for good news for years, so U of L wanted to promote this new scholarship. It would encourage others to once again trust and donate to the U of L Foundation, and it further enhanced U of L's image as a national top twenty-five LGBTQ-friendly institution.

For those reasons, the university engaged its communications team and launched a campaign to raise awareness about the new scholarship. Local media received the news favorably, and it also got picked up by some national publications, including a feature article in the Jesuit magazine *America*. After *USA Today* also had published a story about it, to our pleasant surprise, numerous people around the country decided they wanted to make contributions to the endowment without even being asked.

The last thing Michael and I wanted was press because, as it says in the Bible, when giving alms it's best not to let your left hand know what your right hand is doing. U of L seemed determined to promote the endowment, so we followed its lead. All Michael and I wanted to do was offer hope to LGBTQ Catholics so they wouldn't give up on their faith. The goal was to encourage people to continue working through spiritual and Church-related challenges they might be experiencing, just as we had done. LGBTQ Catholics need that encouragement to remain in the faith and not feel like they have to choose between their identity as LGBTQ or Catholic. The Church can handle people with complex lives.

More proof of progress within the Church came on February 23, 2019. I had for a while been writing cards and notes of prayerful support to Archbishop Kurtz, and we had settled into a quiet period of distant but mutual respect. My generous husband also made sure to make a substantial donation each year to the Archbishop's Annual Catholic Services Appeal. I suppose that didn't hurt. I might be able to come up with fresh words to describe one unexpected incident, but I don't think they'd be as expressive as a Facebook post I made that cold winter night after Saturday evening Mass:

> Tonight we arrived at church and were surprised to see all the cars in the parking lot. We thought it would be our regular quick Saturday night Mass, and we had someplace to be right after church.
>
> We got inside and realized tonight we were having Confirmation for our Lourdes school students and Archbishop Kurtz was celebrating. Given my history with Archbishop I was nervous and intrigued to see how the evening would play out given that I was scheduled to be in the sanctuary with him and serving as a Communion Minister.
>
> Of course I was wearing my rainbow lapel cross. When I entered the sanctuary at Communion he seemed a bit startled but still unfazed. He gave me Communion then passed me my plate to serve from with the other priests. No drama, just joint service to God and Church.
>
> As I passed out Communion I wish I could have videotaped all the smiles and smirks I got from my fellow Lourdes parishioners as we were sharing Communion. They understood the significance of my serving as a Communion Minister with Archbishop Kurtz in that setting, and they were as satisfied and pleased as I was. Praise God for their glory.

That night it felt like all of us—we, he, Michael and I, and the Archdiocese—had all moved beyond much of the petty bickering of the past. As we served Communion, it felt like we were actually in communion. I felt an astounding sense of peace and contentment. Reflecting on that evening, I know there is hope for our Church. We can all move toward the center aisle, meet one another there, and join hands. Together, our Church and its people really can build the bridge about which Father James Martin preaches. Bridges only get built, though, when people invest and actually do the work to build them.

43

NOTRE DAME LAW FORUM

In late 2018, a friend of mine, Katelyn Ringrose, was president of the Notre Dame LGBT Law Forum when she reached out to me about a potential panel. She wanted to know if Michael and I would be interested in participating in an event on campus at the law school to discuss the *Obergefell* case.

As a Notre Dame graduate and longtime member of the GALA ND/ SMC alumni group, I couldn't take a pass on that opportunity. There was still so much resistance back at Notre Dame to inclusion and compassionate treatment of LGBTQ people. This event was guaranteed to bring out both supporters and detractors on the issue of same-sex marriage.

Notre Dame still had many quite conservative people in prominent roles throughout the institution. When it considered moving toward progressive positions, it was ultrasensitive to the implications they might have on donor relations.

On campus over the last ten years or so, the debate over LGBTQ rights and inclusion had intensified at what many consider America's pre-eminent Catholic institution of higher learning. Many conservatives thought Notre Dame had an obligation to defend the Faith and enforce what are often vague and inconsistent Church policies. On the other hand, because it's a prominent institution of higher learning, it also attracts a large number of highly intelligent and quite progressive people to its campus.

As we continued to discuss the upcoming ND LGBT Law Forum, Katelyn and her colleagues decided it would be most effective if Jim

Obergefell could also appear. When Jim agreed, the planning started in earnest. We set a date of March 28, 2019. The LGBT Law Forum decided a panel presentation would work best. ND law professor Pat Hackett would be the moderator.

In the days leading up to the panel, there was both support for and condemnation of the event throughout campus and in the ND student newspaper, *The Observer*. A few days beforehand, *The Observer* published a lengthy letter to the editor asking why Notre Dame was "rolling out the red carpet" for Jim Obergefell. It was particularly critical of the university for allowing people to speak who "openly and proudly reject the Church's teachings on marriage because the costs of orthodoxy are greater than the benefits."

The letter sparked a heated discussion between people who backed the writer and those who challenged the assumptions and arguments behind the letter. The next day, members of the LGBT Law Forum provided their own response in the form of another letter to *The Observer*. It explained the importance of the *Obergefell* ruling as "one of the most legally and socially relevant cases in recent history." The LGBT Forum defended its right to provide a broad range of "scholarly discussions related to legal issues related to lesbian, gay, bisexual and transgender (LGBT) individuals." The Forum's letter was well crafted collaboratively by several future attorneys. Their defense was extremely persuasive. That thoughtful response helped calm the building controversy over the panel.

As is often the case when Michael and I are walking into the spotlight, I started to think about worst-case scenarios. Would some deranged religious fanatic show up with a gun and decide to start taking us all out? What about protestors blocking the entrance to the law school as people tried to get in? Would people in the audience start shouting us down in protest as we tried to speak? Honestly, I could envision any of that happening at that place and under those circumstances.

As has pretty much always been the case in my activist endeavors, those fears proved to be unfounded. The panel discussion went off without a hitch. The crowd filled the auditorium. An overflow room displayed the discussion on video. To our pleasant surprise, the crowd was dignified and respectful of the panelists and the stories we had to tell. It was an important day on the Notre Dame campus to have this type of visibility and a civil discussion on a topic that still very much divides many Catholics.

44

TIME TO REFLECT

When my mother passed in 2019 on Good Friday evening, six hours before her ninety-third birthday, it left a great hole my heart. For years I'd spent much of my spare time making sure Dad and Mom were taken good care of. Thank God for my three brothers, who also all live in Louisville and did the same. Over the years we all shared the duties of paying back our dues to parents for all they'd done for us growing up and through the decades.

After Mom was gone, God started pestering me once again about sitting down and writing out these thoughts, questioning what I was going to use as my next excuse for not heeding the call to share the good news. In the spring of 2019, when my visits to Mom ended, it was time to finally respond to the call and start reflecting deeply on my sometimes painful past. I determined I needed to omit much of the really difficult and controversial content. This message was meant to be about the triumph of faith over persecution.

As I'm finishing up this writing in late 2020, Michael and I, with a devoted core of progressive fellow parishioners, are in the process of launching an LGBTQ ministry at Our Lady of Lourdes Catholic Church. For more than a year we have been coordinating efforts to launch this ministry. There is only one other formal LGBTQ ministry at a Catholic church in Kentucky, and no others in our part of the country. After having been members at Lourdes for thirty-three years, this will be new territory for us and the parish.

Ironically, a few of our straight ally parishioners, such as Stephen Heitz and Tricia Fike Lewis, have been driving its development, along with our worship director, Gregory Dupont. This couldn't be more satisfying. Although our pastor has been supportive, we are a bit concerned about how the Archdiocese might ultimately respond to a ministry of this nature if it starts getting public attention beyond the parish. It's a little unclear if or how successful this effort will be, but we do know there is an appetite for it.

There are still so many LGBTQ youth being disowned, thrown out of homes, and otherwise discarded by misguided parents who think they're responding in a manner consistent with God's desires by condemning these people. They are wrong, and I have a message to all parents, one that I have learned myself as a parent and from reflecting frequently on the parable of the Prodigal Son. Take it from someone who has been on both sides of that parable, both the prodigal son and the parent of the prodigal son. That parable provides the most powerful parent–child relationship advice you can get.

So here's my message to you:

Parents, please simply love your children no matter what. Remember all the regrettable things that you have done, when you have sinned or otherwise strayed from God's path. Remember how comforting it was when you realized that God was patiently waiting for you to come back and always loved you no matter what. God's love for us is unconditional and no one can take that away, not even can we take it away from ourselves because God's love endures forever. So, please love your children when they "come out" to you with whatever it is they have to say. God would not reject them, so why would you? Remember that both Jesus and Pope Francis have instructed us not to judge others. That is not your job. Your job is to love one another, including your children, no matter what.

We have just marked the five-year anniversary of the Supreme Court ruling in *Obergefell v. Hodges*, so it's a good time to consider what has not happened since the decision. The world has not come to a screeching halt. The Catholic Church is still quite strong despite its many challenges. People of all combinations of genders, gender identities, and gender expression have continued to get married. The world seems to be a better place because of the freedom that Americans now finally have to marry the person they love.

The life that Michael and I have shared for the last thirty-eight years has not been easy, but no one I've ever met has told me their life was easy. That's just part of the human condition. We are all put here to struggle and fail and overcome. In the process of living, we have lessons to both learn and teach.

I am now sixty-three, and I've been generally satisfied with the outcomes from my time on this planet. Like everyone I have a few regrets about things I've done or haven't done. On many occasions I didn't do very well. But before my time on this planet is through, there are a couple of things I would like to see.

First, I'd like to see the Catholic Church give up on its crusade against LGBTQ people, open its doors wide, and welcome them in. Absent that, it seems warranted that the Church could offer a simple apology for its past persecution of LGBTQ people. An official apology would start to reconcile for all the pain Church policies have caused the LGBTQ community in the past.

Speaking of apologies, the Lincoln Heritage Council and the Boy Scouts of America owe an apology to my pastor, Father Scott Wimsett. When I was ousted, I was treated pretty cruelly by the BSA. But Father Scott was an innocent victim. He had to take the brunt of the LHC's intimidation when they threatened him with closing the Boy Scout unit at Lourdes if I wasn't forced out. That type of behavior was inexcusable. Although I have apologized to Father Scott for his ill-treatment in those events, he deserves an apology from an organization that is supposed to stand for the Scout principles of courtesy and kindness.

45

WHAT WOULD THAT EVEN LOOK LIKE?

Many Catholics over the years have struggled with the issue of LGBTQ people and how to treat them. The wide range has run from damnation and excommunication to marginalization to tolerance to full inclusion. Currently, our Church seems to be stuck somewhere between marginalization and tolerance. There are still many Catholics who would fall anywhere on the continuum.

How is it that a Church that is supposed to be One Church can have so much variation on a single topic? There are other issues in the Church, such as divorce or women serving as deacons or priests, which have also been quite divisive over the years. But no issue seems to have produced so much inconsistency among Catholics as how to handle LGBTQ people and especially what to do about same-sex marriage.

Today, the Church will not even allow itself to consider the possibility of same-sex marriage and is fighting it in theory and practice at every turn. Most recently it has fired many employees who have even a whiff of being gay and married or engaged. This fear is irrational. It reeks of oppression and discrimination. It very much damages the image of the Church in the eyes of people who already view it as acting in a petty and vindictive manner.

Since the Church is having so much trouble trying to figure out "what would that even look like" to have same-sex married people integrated into Catholic communities, allow me to provide a little insight.

Imagine two people who meet while attending college and try to better themselves by growing and developing academically. Pretty much immediately they fall in love and become inseparable. They start doing everything together, including going to Mass every weekend. After they figure out they belong together, this couple makes a commitment and moves in together. After completing their higher education, they embark on a new life. They move far away to start their professional careers, all the while continuing to worship together and celebrating their relationship with God. After a few years away, the draw of their family lures them into moving back to their home state. They buy a suburban house, settle down, and immediately join a Catholic parish a block and a half away.

After time passes, they decide that they're ready to have a family, but since they're not able to have them biologically, they adopt two children. They raise them in the Church, send them to Catholic schools from preschool through high school, and make sure they receive all of their sacraments and proper religious formation along the way.

Picture this couple over many decades. They participate in numerous ministries at their parish, including soccer coach, Communion minister, parish council, Boy Scout leader, ground maintenance, Girl Scout leader, Resurrection Choir, Knights of Columbus, and Worship Committee. Envision this couple working together as volunteers at Lenten fish fries and parish summer picnics for decades side by side other parishioners. Think of this couple as not only faithful stewards of time and talent but practitioners of tithing who also donate financially to a wide range of other worthy causes outside of the parish.

Imagine this couple. It could be any two people. But why would it have to be two people of the opposite gender? Is it so hard for the Church and its people to look at the possibilities of what same-sex marriage might look like and consider how that might actually be wholly consistent with Church values and teachings? To any in the Church who think it can never accept same-sex married couples into its fold, tell me, please, what is so offensive about people who live good lives, do good work, and live in, love, and support their Church?

This has been our life together. The people at our parish, Our Lady of Lourdes, get it. They have grown over our thirty-three years as active parishioners at Lourdes to see us just like any other couple. They welcome us as part of a diverse and inclusive faith community. Michael and I are legally married, and we are Catholic, and we will remain both until death do us part.

That, to me, is the real meaning of the fullness of charity.

INDEX

photo shoot prior to Supreme
Court hearing, 115
plaintiff reception prior to Supreme
Court hearing, 115–16
the Sixth Circuit hearing and,
88–89, 93–95
the Sixth Circuit reversal and,
100–104
at Supreme Court oral arguments,
117–23
Yale Law Review article on plaintiffs
being "cast," 160–61
attorneys (*Obergefell v. Hodges*
lawsuit)
ACLU supporting, during Supreme
Court case, 117, 124
celebrating Supreme Court victory,
144–45
following Supreme Court decision,
138–39
following Supreme Court oral
arguments, 123–24
photo shoot prior to Supreme
Court hearing, 115
plaintiff reception prior to Supreme
Court hearing, 115–16
at Supreme Court oral arguments,
117–23
Yale Law Review article on plaintiffs
being "cast," 160–61
Ayers, Geordie, 74

baptism, 178
of Bryson, 24–25
of Isaiah, 26
Bar, The (Lexington gay bar), 5–6
Barlow, Luke, 70–71
Barr, Mac, 46–47
BBC News, 128
Beck, Andrew, 13
Bendapudi, Neeli, 197

Bergen, Jack, 183–84
Beshear, Bourke v. (marriage equality
lawsuit). See *Bourke v. Beshear*
Beshear, Love v. (marriage equality
lawsuit), 82, 87–88
Beshear, Steve, 72, 80, 82, 83–85, 93.
See also *Bourke v. Beshear*
(marriage equality lawsuit)
Bickford, Justin, 60
Biden, Joe, 145
Blanchard, Maurice, 76–77, 81–82,
117
Bohn, Denise, 196
Bonauto, Mary, 123, 138, 140–41, 145
Bourke, Gaye (Greg's aunt), 16
Bourke, Greg
childhood of, 2, 8, 149
coming-out process, 5, 10, 12, 17, 20
early years of dating, 6–10
education of, 5, 7, 11, 55, 129, 163,
170
employment at Brandeis
Machinery, 15
employment at Humana, 20–21,
107, 150
employment at Irving B. Moore
Corporation, 11
faith of, 2, 5, 6–7, 13, 18, 45, 128,
168–69, 185–86
family celebrations, 106, 129
family life and parenting, 24–26,
31, 91, 157
family minivan, 113
family relationships, 9–10, 21,
188–89, 190
family role models, 7–8
family vacations, 86–87, 115
fears experienced by, 31–32, 110–11,
125, 201
friendships with other gay
Catholics, 13, 14

discrimination (*cont.*)
workplace discrimination, 20–21,
186, 205
See also Boy Scouts of America
(BSA); marriage equality
movement
Disney, 86
divorce, 122, 156
DOMA (Defense of Marriage Act,
1996), 63–64, 105, 131
Donahue, Phil, 183, 184, 185, 186–87
Downey, Andy, 69
Dunaway, Allan, 182
Dunman, Joe, 74, 94, 100, 105, 118
Dupont, Gregory, 203

Eagle Scout rank (BSA)
Eagle Mentor pins, 74, 194–95
Greg as Eagle Project coach, 53,
129, 159, 194–95
Isaiah's Board of Review, 70
Isaiah's Court of Honor ceremony,
74
Isaiah's service project for, 53,
58–59
Ryan Andresen denied, 52
elementary school (Lourdes), 18, 27,
31
Ellen DeGeneres Show, 52
Elliott, Dawn
district court case, 66–69, 72–73
expanding legal team, 74
helping with second-parent
adoption process, 181
Judge Heyburn's ruling and, 78–85
possible lawsuit against BSA, 146
the Sixth Circuit hearing and, 90
on the Sixth Circuit's reversal, 102
at the Supreme Court hearing, 118
employment discrimination, 20–21,
186, 205

Equal Protection Clause (Fourteenth
Amendment)
purpose of, 83, 88, 126
quasi-suspect classes under, 87–88
state constitutional bans violating,
63, 80–81, 82, 87–88, 104
Equal Scouting movement, 60–62,
71–72
Esseks, James, 128, 130, 132, 133, 138,
139, 145
Eucharistic Prayer, 1–2

Fairness Campaign (LGBTQ rights
organization)
celebrating Supreme Court victory,
145
Kentucky's same-sex marriage ban
and, 28–29
lobbying for marriage equality, 101
lobbying Metro United Way
(MUW), 54–55, 96
protesting the Archdiocesan
memorial approval process,
175–76
supporting Greg's advocacy for
equality in scouting, 51, 54–55,
96, 153
Fairness Ordinance (1999), 20–21
Fajardo, Javier, 174
Fauver, Shannon
district court case, 66–69, 72–73
expanding legal team, 74
filing Supreme Court petition,
104–5
helping with second-parent
adoption process, 181
and Judge Heyburn's ruling, 78–85
possible lawsuit against BSA, 146
preparing for Supreme Court filing,
103
the Sixth Circuit hearing and, 90

the Sixth Circuit reversal and, 100, 103
  at the Supreme Court hearing, 118
Felker, Tracie, 60
Ferraro, Rich, 52
Fischer, Greg, 145
Fisher, Jeffrey, 108, 145
Fourteenth Amendment (U.S. Constitution)
  purpose of, 83, 88, 126, 135
  quasi-suspect classes under, 87–88
  state constitutional bans violating, 63, 80–81, 82, 87–88, 104
  Supreme Court's consideration of, 106–7
Francis (pope), 158, 169, 184, 203
Franklin, Kim, 68, 70–71
Freedom to Marry (organization)
  celebrating Supreme Court victory, 145
  on possible Supreme Court case outcomes, 129–30
  profiling marriage equality plaintiffs, 89
  reception hosted by, 109, 115–16
  supporting Supreme Court marriage equality case, 102–3, 108, 129–30

GALA ND/SMC (Gay and Lesbian Alumni of Notre Dame/Saint Mary's College)
  lack of official recognition, 128–29, 148–49, 164, 177
  LGBTQ scholarship benefit, 183–84, 186–87
  Reunion Weekend panel, 128–29, 177
Gates, Robert, 127, 147
gay bars, 5–6, 110
General Electric (GE), 20, 22, 65, 84

Gerhardstein, Alphonse "Al," 93, 138
Ginsburg, Ruth Bader, 120, 121, 122, 135
Girl Scouts (Lourdes), 42, 151, 155
GLAAD (formerly the Gay and Lesbian Alliance Against Defamation)
  activism targeting BSA's antigay policies, 52, 56–59, 150
  and the Catholic Persons of the Year award, 168
  at the Equal Scouting Summit (2013), 61
  and Greg's *OUT* magazine photo shoot, 71–72
  work with Scouts for Equality, 52, 60–61
Golden, Joanne, 189
Golden, Tim, 189
Grand, Steve, 75

Hackett, Pat, 201
Hall, Warren, 186
Hallward-Driemeier, Douglas, 120–22, 123, 138
Hankins, Brad, 57, 60, 61, 127
Harbison, William L., 93
Harry, Debra, 76
Hartford (CT), 11–14
Hartman, Chris
  the annual Catholics for Fairness rally and, 170
  celebrating *Windsor* ruling, 64
  meeting with Archbishop Kurtz, 154–56
  in the "Pilgrimage of Mercy" rally, 184–85, 186
  protesting the Archdiocesan memorial approval process, 175–76
  relationship with Greg, 54–55

GREG BOURKE

has had a long corporate career in information technology and management. He currently works as a health economist. Bourke and his husband, Michael De Leon, were named 2015 Persons of the Year by the National Catholic Reporter and have been active in establishing LGBTQ alumni networks at the University of Notre Dame, University of Louisville, University of Kentucky, and other organizations.